The Art of Palmistry

Also by Ray Douglas:

    Palmistry and the Inner Self
    Teach Yourself Palmistry
    The Handbook of Palmistry

The Art of

Palmistry

by

Ray Douglas

ISBN 978-1-907091-05-6

First published in the UK in 1998 by Hodder & Stoughton as *Palmistry*. This edition with amendments and additions published in 2009 by Dreamstairway

Copyright © 1998 & 2009 Ray Douglas

www.dreamstairway.co.uk

CONTENTS

1 **First principles of palmistry**   p9
   What is palmistry?   p9
   Where and how did it originate?   p9
   How can palmistry work?   p10
   Conscious energies and unconscious influences   p13
   An individual source of power   p16
   Directions of movement   p17
   The main lines of the hand   p19
   The Rascette   p19

2 **The mounts**   p21
   The background of personality   p21
   Planetary rulership   p21
   The significance of the mounts   p24
   The Mount of Jupiter   p26
   The Mount of Saturn   p27
   The Mount of the Sun   p28
   The Mount of Mercury   p29
   The Mount of Venus   p30
   The Lower Mount of Mars   p31
   The Mount of the Moon   p33
   The Upper Mount of Mars   p34

3 **Cheirognomy: Hands, fingers and thumbs**   p35
   The cheirotype   p35
   Fingers   p39
   Thumbs   p46
   Fingerprints   p49
   The full picture   p51

4 **The Heart Line**   p53
   The flow of feelings   p53
   The rising point   p56
   Signs on the Heart Line   p60
   Links with the Head Line   p64

5 The Head Line   p67
   The flow of thoughts p67
   The physical basis of thought p70
   Tielines and signs p74

6 The Life Line   p78
   Physical energy p78
   Timescales p81
   Lines of Influence p84
   Other signs on the Life Line p87

7 The Line of Fate   p88
   Timing the events of fate p88
   Divergence of fate p93

8 The Line of Fortune   p96
   Success and self-regard p96

9 The Line of Intuition   p102
   The third impersonal influence p102

10 Love and marriage   p106
   Affectionate relationships p106
   The Girdle of Venus p109
   Difficult births p111
   The quality of marriage p112

11 Health and excess   p120
   A line of ill-health p120

12 Sympathy and sensitivity   p125
   Caring hands p125

13 Influence and dominance   p130
   Lines of Influence p130
   Lines of Dominance p134

14 Adventure and misadventure   p136
   Safe journeys p136
   Warning signs p139

15 **Left hand – right hand** p141
   Inheritance p141
   Material and abstract p145

16 **Summary of human characteristics** p146
   Aggression p146
   Ambition p147
   Assertiveness p148
   Creativity p149
   Depression p150
   Faithfulness p152
   Fickleness p152
   Introspection p153
   Jealousy p154
   Kindness p155
   Moodiness p156
   Resourcefulness p157
   Self-confidence p159

17 **Summary of vocational signs** p160
   Accountant p160
   Actor p160
   Architect p160
   Artist p161
   Athlete p161
   Banker p161
   Builder 162
   Chemist p162
   Church minister p162
   Clerical officer p163
   Computer programmer p163
   Cook p163
   Doctor p163
   Draftsperson p164
   Driver (bus or lorry) p164
   Engineer p164
   Farmer p165
   Fashion designer p165
   Forester p165
   Hospital administrator p166
   Hotel manager p166

Journalist p166
Kennel or stable worker p167
Lawyer p167
Librarian p167
Motor mechanic p167
Novelist p168
Nurse p168
Police officer p168
Politician p169
Publisher p169
Radio or television presenter p169
Salesperson p170
Secretary p170
Social welfare worker p170
Soldier p171
Teacher p171
Veterinary surgeon p171

18 Points to consider when giving readings p172
   Age and peace of mind p172

Index   p176

1
FIRST PRINCIPLES OF PALMISTRY

What is palmistry?

Palmistry is not a science, nor is it a pseudo-science. Palmistry is an art: the art of using the hand, or both hands taken together, to symbolise the whole person. It is also known as cheiromancy or chiromancy (from the Greek *cheiro* — hand, and *manteia* — divination). There is also that branch of palmistry known as cheirognomy, which concerns mainly the shape and general appearance of the hand (Greek *gnome* — understanding). The two branches of the art are nowadays best blended into one.

The hand, complete with all its lines and minor marks or signs, is taken as representative of its owner, and symbolises his or her life and character at whatever level of understanding you may wish to pursue and study it. Because it is about the whole person, palmistry can concern itself equally with erudite matters of the psyche, or with everyday trivia; it can soar with the mind of its interpreter to all the heights to which intellectual or spiritual sensitivities may aspire, or with equal facility it may 'wallow in the mire of bodily lust'. It is ourselves, wherever we are, and wherever we want to be.

Where and how did it originate?

It is likely that palmistry was used regularly in prehistoric society. Certainly it is known to have been practised in China five thousand years ago, and frequently it has featured in some of the most ancient known literature of the world. Besides the Chinese, the ancient Greeks, Romans, Egyptians, Hebrews, Arabs and Chaldeans all had long traditions of palmistry, as do the Indians and Malays.

To most of these ancients, perhaps, palmistry has been revered as a science. Today, sensible palmists make no claim to scientific status. Ancient science is often enough seen to have been ancient nonsense. Today, we understand better how to use the art of palmistry so that it does have real meaning. Early European works such as the Italian *Chiromantia* of 1531, the German *Die Kunst Ciromancia* of 1545, or the English *Book of Palmestry* of 1651, themselves largely refinements of the somewhat chaotic ancient literature covering the subject, contain the first elements of organisation and standardisation of palmistry into the form we know today, though many of their authors' observations may seem to us to have been irrational or even absurd.

During the intervening centuries serious palmists have been continually adding to that basic information through detailed observation. That said, however, any attempt to make a science of the subject is to make nonsense of it. As an art, palmistry is full of fascinating discoveries and revealing insights. In this role, it has a real and abiding value in the world today.

How can palmistry work?

What exactly *are* the lines of the hand? And why should they mean anything? In anatomical terms, the outer skin or epidermis over most of our body tends to be fairly loosely arranged over the deeper layers of the cuticle or 'true skin'. When you rub your body the skin tends to move about. But the chief function of the palm of the hand is to grasp, and if the skin on that part of the body were unstable, we would not be able to grip firmly and efficiently.

The skin of the palm also needs to flex or bend very neatly and tightly along with the movements of grasping, as when we clench our fists. In order to fulfil these functions efficiently the flexion folds throughout their length are firmly tied by connecting fibres, or fibrillar tissue, to the deep layers of the dermis, and to the sheaths of the flexor tendons. These folding lines, or *sulci*, form the distinctive and clearly marked lines with which we are familiar. They are further emphasised by subcutaneous layers of fat arranged between them, which serve to pad the skin so as both to strengthen the grip and at the same time to protect the underlying tendons from damage. These raised areas are known anatomically as the *monticuli*, in palmistry as the mounts.

Thus the fixed, permanent lines on our hand are not formed haphazardly in the womb by the fist-clenching of the foetus; they are arranged in a fairly consistent pattern common to the whole human race. In each individual, to a greater or lesser degree, they vary enough to show individuality in a pattern already decided for us at our conception by our parents' and our ancestors' genes.

Genetic abnormalities which may affect the personality often have physical signs which a doctor will recognise. But the normal range of personalities and the happenings of fate, though obvious enough during life, have an abstract nature. They cannot be plotted physically; they cannot be dissected or discovered during a *post mortem* examination. Their only real proof is their experience. You are unlikely to succeed in proving the validity of palmistry through a process of logic, any more than that of religious faith. A sceptic might demand to know, for example, what and where precisely is the connection between the Head Line and the mental processes? Or where is the neurological link between the emotional centre of the brain and the Heart Line? And, of course, this sceptical type of question will get no sensible answer.

But if you study your own hand in the light of your own knowledge of yourself, and the hands of your family and friends in the light of your knowledge of them, you will very soon say: 'It really does work!' It all comes back to the distinction between art and science: art, like personality, has an abstract base; science, like the physical body, has a material one. The art of palmistry works chiefly through symbolism and synchronicity. As a uniquely personal map carried by each individual, a pattern which corresponds with a person's past and present life, the hand can equally well provide a forecast of routes to be taken, of probabilities for the future.

It used to be thought that personality was largely decided by a person's upbringing, but this turns out not to be true. Personality is decided almost entirely, not by environment, but by our genes. Academic studies on identical twins who have been separated since birth have demonstrated this fact quite conlusively. Their hand patterns, we can assume, will be very similar, and when these twins have finally been brought together in middle age, the researchers have discovered that their lifestyles, health, mannerisms, and their patterns of speech, habits of thinking and feeling, are all virtually identical too. Even the things that have happened to them during their years apart, good fortune and misfortune alike, major events which might have been put down to mere chance, have also corresponded to an uncanny degree. When twins grow up together, of course, they often strive to be different, and usually succeed — but normally in a way that does not show up in the three major lines.

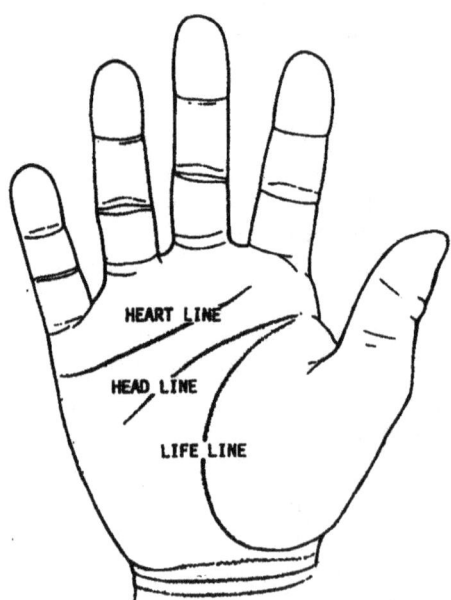

Figure 1

The three principal lines

FIRST PRINCIPLES OF PALMISTRY

Conscious energies and unconscious influences

If you study your own hands you may notice that, while the three main firmly tied-down lines are clearly recognisable, there is another type of line that may or may not be present in the individual palm. This second category consists of lines that are *not* tied to the deep layers, or tied only very lightly, so that unlike the fixed lines they could be said to be to some degree haphazardly disposed, though they too will be found to follow a fairly precise pattern. They form a sort of lateral or transverse counter-movement to the straightforward gripping function catered for by the main, permanent lines.

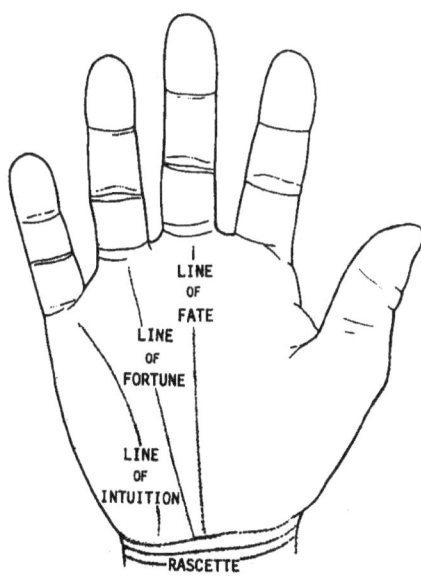

Figure 2

The three secondary lines

The most distinct and deeply anchored lines, then, are the personal lines fixed and decided for you by your genes. As permanent and unique symbols of your personal inheritance, from the viewpoint of palmistry they can be seen as tracks along which your will and actions, the quality of your thoughts and emotions, your physical vigour and habitual lifestyle, may be said to flow. The unfixed or only lightly fixed lines, which tend to run up the length of the palm from the wrist towards the base of the fingers, have a different connotation to the palmist. Being to a large extent acquired not through the genes but apparently by chance, brought about by transient or at least less permanent factors, these secondary lines form apposite symbols of the uninherited, impersonal influences that sometimes arise quite unexpectedly to affect our lives.

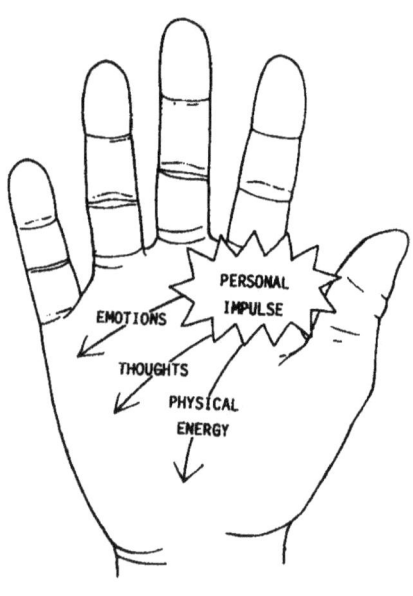

Figure 3   Streams of consciousness

Individual palms vary greatly in the intensity of these secondary lines; in some case they are strongly marked, in others very faint or lacking altogether. To the extent that some of these transverse or ascending lines are, however, fixed and permanent, the implication is that in the individual case, and during the individual lifetime, fate itself is fixed and permanent. The difference between the two sorts of lines represents the difference between what is inborn in the individual and what is not. In broader terms it can be said that the function, influence or impulse symbolised by a fixed line is fixed and permanent during the life of its owner. The lines that are not permanently fixed represent those factors that time and circumstances may change. Together, they can give us an idea of the day-to-day fate to be encountered during our lifetime, and our probable reactions to all these factors.

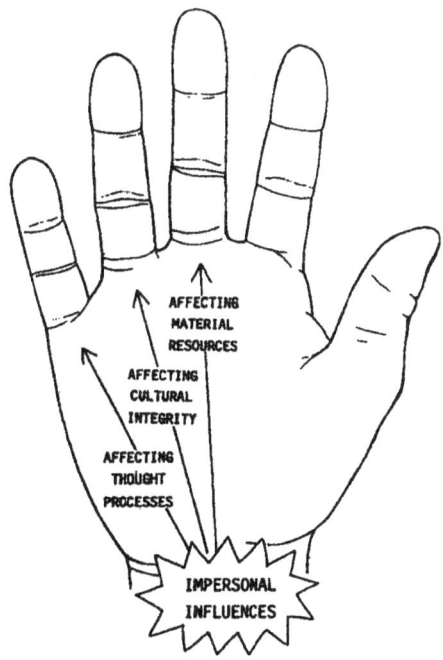

Figure 4

Impulses from the unconscious mind

An individual source of power

A study of palmistry is best begun with a general appraisal of the map of the hand. The important thing is to understand, or at least to appreciate, the broad principles of palmistry, and the underlying law of cause and effect, before tackling all the fine details. A basic grounding such as this is really what distinguishes the serious palmist from a mere dabbler in the art, although, as we have already seen, there are many differing levels of understanding involved in reading the hand. Palmists, too, may vary in their interests: from the simple search for 'luck', from the psychic using the hand as an inspiration, to the seeker after inner values.

To the palmist not only the lines but the mounts between them, too, reflect the pattern of individual thoughts and emotions, and habitual individual methods of facing and surmounting life's situations during times good and bad. The diagrams show the right hand. Study your own right palm and notice in particular the area immediately beneath the index or pointing finger. This small area — one of the mounts — is an important point in the palm, for it represents a power-source for each human individual. Everything personal and conscious and belonging to the realm of the psyche can be said to emanate from this area, because from this mount, or close to it, the major fixed lines sweep across and down the palm. From this zone of personal energy, streams of consciousness visualised as being channelled by the fixed lines also run outwards and downwards.

Topmost is the stream of emotions, the feelings; centrally, the flow of thoughts; lowermost and downwards-curving runs the course of bodily sensations, the channel of physical energy, the personal life force. These movements operate within normal consciousness, within individual awareness, representing the workings of the logical brain, the emotional feelings, and the physical being: the whole practical course of life. As streams of consciousness, they correspond with the three main 'fixed' lines of the hand.

Directions of movement

Carrying the principle a little further, it can be seen that the palm of the hand may be divided into broad areas of concern, each particularly relevant to a type of psychic function. On the side of the thumb — itself the manipulative symbol of humanity having risen above the brute beasts — we have the zone of objectivity, the physical, concrete and tangible ways of thinking and acting. On the side of the little finger is its counterpart: the area that is concerned with all that is subjective, abstract and intangible.

At the top of the palm, at the base of the fingers, is the area of conscious awareness, a register of the clearly recognisable categories of life, or the human qualities which make up the personality. Beneath the whole field of the conscious as symbolised by the palm itself, at the wrist we can visualise the zone of the impersonal, the largely unknown territory from which spring all the influences and spontaneous ideas that may affect our thinking and behaviour, and yet do not seem to be the product of our own thinking and feeling. Whether this source of influence is visualised as within or external to the human psyche, it is what is known as the 'collective unconscious'.

It can now be seen that the hand shows two directions or tides of movement in individual human affairs: those factors which arise from the will — the conscious, deliberate actions — and those which arise spontaneously and unconsciously, without the power of will. This latter type of occurrence includes the impersonal, unwilled happenings of fate, intuition, and 'luck', things which just seem to happen without our intentions. The former category stems from consciousness, from personal awareness and intent, from physical being, from the workings of the brain, the emotional feelings, and the practical everyday course of life. The latter category stems from the realm of the unconscious mind. All in all, the two directions of movement mark the difference between what is inborn, and what is imposed and impersonal.

The diagrams show how these impersonal influences may

be depicted on the hand. The influences which do not arise from the will and include all the unexpected happenings of chance: fate, good or bad 'luck', flashes of intuition or deeper insight, meaningful dreams or visions; when these things happen they do so despite our expectations or intentions. Such impersonal influences also tend to adhere to three distinct streams of movement. They comprise in turn those factors which make their presence known in the sphere of physical, material resources; those which affect the cultural integrity and emotional well-being of the individual; and those which affect and influence the processes of thinking and understanding.

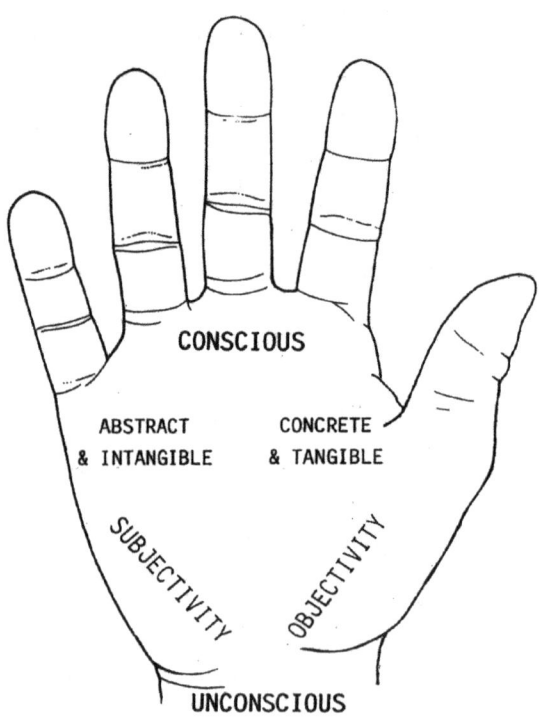

Figure 5   Psychic zones

FIRST PRINCIPLES OF PALMISTRY

The main lines of the hand

If you have followed the thread so far, it will have become plain that there are six major lines, divided between the fixed and the unfixed, between those arising from the conscious and those arising from unconscious mind. The three primary or tied lines represent the three conscious or personal functions: emotional feeling, with the Heart Line; thinking, or intellectual quality, with the Head Line; and physical sensation, health and strength, with the Life Line. In the symbolism of palmistry these three lines register the nature, the direction and the quality of emotions and thoughts, and the vigour and quality of a person's physical life (page 12).

The three secondary lines representing the three unconscious or impersonal functions are: the Line of Fate, carrying with it a material or physical connotation; the Line of Fortune, connected with matters of prestige, culture and personal integrity; and the Line of Intuition, seen as a channel for those flashes of revelation or illogical hunches which may spring to the mind without warning (page 13). Always remember in which direction the main lines 'go': the Heart, Head and Life Lines start near the base of the index finger; the Lines of Fate, Fortune and Intuition start near the wrist.

The Rascette

The wrist itself is characterised, typically, by three rings known anatomically as the *rasceta,* in palmistry as the Rascette, popularly called the bracelets. They could be thought of in symbolic terms as a dam holding back the full flow of influences from the unconscious mind — the sea of collective human life — a dam which is penetrated or piped by the three secondary lines of impersonal influence, channelling their intermittent flow. They are shown in the diagrams on pages 12 and 13. Individuals who have three clearly defined, unbroken bracelets on both wrists may well have as their motto *mens sana in corpore sano,* a healthy mind in a healthy body, for they are sure to be healthy, well-balanced, down-to-earth people untroubled by 'images from the unconscious mind' or any other fanciful notions. But when the Rascette rings are blurred and indistinct, the implication is rather the opposite: such people may be physically healthy, but they never seem quite sure where or how they are to fit into the world. Their grip on concrete reality is not quite so firm.

There are a few special 'signs' that may appear on the lines of the Rascette, and when they do they are given traditional significance by the palmist. The topmost ring of the Rascette in particular is liable to show a 'chained' formation, as though made up of a series of small links or circles. These are said to represent the numerous small problems that most people have to face in their lives. A larger configuration on the topmost ring, like an island in a river, signifies a considerable handicap that needs to be overcome in the subject's life, Sometimes, the Rascette lines are broken, as though to breach the 'dam'; occasionally they are marked with a cross, or a star of tiny, fine lines. Their traditional meaning is set out below.

Signs on the Rascette

Star	Happiness in old age. Also the traditional sign of an inheritance or unexpected wealth.
Cross	On or just above the topmost ring: hardship experienced during childhood.
Chain	Relatively minor problems to be overcome.
Island	A considerable problem or handicap that affects the subject's life.
Breaks	Awareness of signals received from the unconscious mind.

2
THE MOUNTS

The background of personality

The lines of the hand, it could be said, trace the course of an individual life through the battlefield of the senses. The mounts, the fleshy, slightly raised areas between the lines, represent that battlefield — the background of personality, the nature and intensity of the passions which are inbuilt within the psyche, and with which the senses interact. The mounts each have their own characteristic nature, and they share their names with the planets.

This may sound familiar to those who have followed their 'stars' in the daily newspapers; but it would be wrong to assume that palmistry includes elements of astrology, or vice versa. Both are ancient systems of psychological analysis, and simply use the same set of terms to identify these inbuilt passions which are common to everybody. The course of any life, whether it be represented by the lines of the hand or by a horoscope, threads its way through and between these characteristics. In astrology they feature as the planets, in palmistry as the mounts.

Planetary rulership

This similarity has led many people to consider the mounts of the hand in terms of planetary rulership, although the actual planets in the sky have nothing whatever to do with the hand. The names by which we know the planets refer to what we might call 'psychic compartments' of the human condition, personalised centuries ago as divine beings who presided over mankind. The planets were named after these characteristics, these ancient gods and goddesses, rather than the other way around. However, the same system and the same set of terms can apply equally to the human condition as to the solar system, because this is what they have come to represent: the whole of humanity or, equally, any individual human being, seen as a microcosm, a miniature version of the solar system, the macrocosm.

In this context the Sun in its relationship with the Earth and the other planets will represent, not 'up' or outwards, but 'down' or inwards, as the vital centre, the spark of life. In planetary terms, the 'influence' of a planet lies within its orbit. The principle applies equally in palmistry: the orbits of Mars, Jupiter, Saturn and the outermost planets all surround that of the Earth. In symbolic terms this means that the influence represented by these planets is greater than the human individual, and we cannot escape them or control them. The orbits of Venus and Mercury, however, are less than the orbit of the Earth: the human individual is greater than his or her

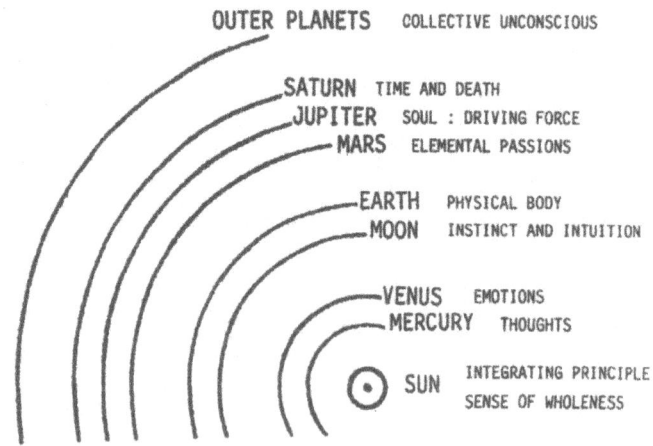

Figure 6

The solar system representing the individual

emotions and thoughts; these things arise through personal development and, to some extent at least, should fall under human control. The moon, as representative of human instincts and intuition, can be greater than thoughts or feelings, or it can be overshadowed by them. It depends upon the individual capacity to receive them and make use of them.

All this may best be seen, perhaps, in diagrammatic form (opposite). Central to the solar system and the nucleus of all planetary orbits, the Sun represents the vital spark, the principle of wholeness, the completion of personality, or self-fulfilment, cultural and psychological integration. Circling the Sun most closely, so that it seems to move very rapidly, is Mercury, personalised as the messenger of the gods — that is, of the other planets — and the symbol of darting thoughts. Surrounding this in turn is the orbit of Venus, symbol of the emotions, in evolutionary terms perhaps not as close to the psychic centre or as exalted as thoughts, but capable nevertheless of great heights and great depths. Next is the orbit of our mother planet Earth, representing our own physical being, with her attendant Moon, symbol of our bodily instincts and impulses, traditional source of imagination and intuition.

Surrounding the 'physical' Earth orbit is the orbit of Mars, the red symbol of fiery elemental passions, the seat of aggression and obsessive, uncontrolled desires, as well as tenacity and determination. These basic passions, don't forget, symbolically surround each whole physical being, complete with his or her own set of instincts, emotions, thoughts, and the central spark of life itself.

There is another essential orbit surrounding these passions and the whole human being: the orbit of Jupiter, representative of the soul. Vastly larger than the inner planets, the soul contains every human possibility within its orbit, and represents a subtle driving force that originates beyond the passions that try to obscure it, vastly higher and broader than the highest and broadest of thoughts and feelings.

Jupiter does not complete the human spectrum, however. There is one factor that surrounds even the soul with its orbit: the limiting principle of Old Father Time or Chronos, represented by the planet Saturn. Time, change and decay, birth and death, these are the factors that control every human being, and the whole human race.

Beyond Saturn, orbits of the outlying planets can be taken to represent the unconscious sea of collective humanity, the source, we can say, of all the impulses and influences which do not arise from the soul and the normal ambitions, the driving passions, the weight of materiality, personal instincts, feelings or thoughts. On the hand, this mysterious zone is symbolised at the wrist by the three rings of the Rascette, the starting point of the lines of impersonal influence, and the symbolic source of all the unexpected happenings of fate.

The significance of the mounts

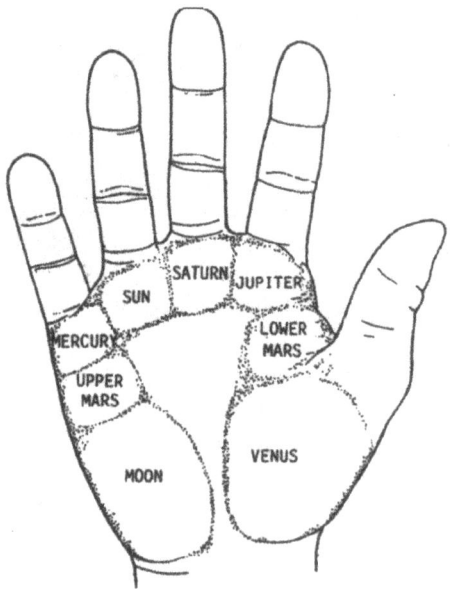

Figure 7

The names of the mounts

THE MOUNTS

The diagrams on these two pages show the traditional names given to the mounts, and the chief characteristics ascribed to them. You will recall that the plan of the hand may be divided into two halves: that concerned with the concrete, material side of the personality, and that concerned with the abstract side. The Mounts of Jupiter, Saturn, Lower Mars and Venus are concrete and material by nature; the Mounts of the Sun, Mercury, Upper Mars and the Moon are abstract. The former set represents *action;* the latter, *reaction*.

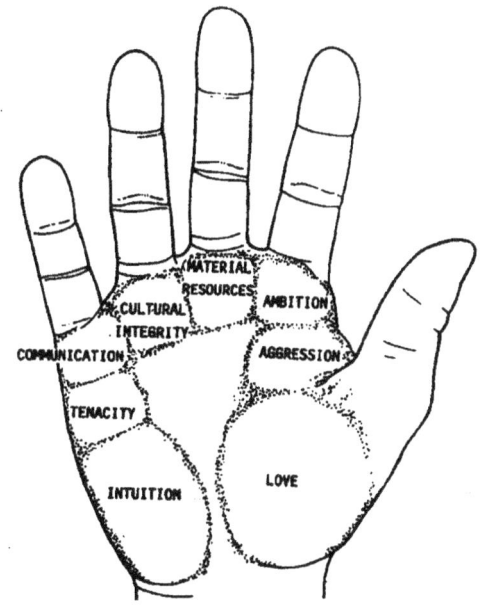

Figure 8

Qualities associated with the mounts

You will also recall that the upper part of the palm, nearest to the fingers, represents the most conscious part of the mind. The further down the palm towards the wrist, in symbolic terms, the closer we are to the unconscious mind. The uppermost mounts therefore: Jupiter, Saturn, Sun and Mercury, may conveniently be known as the mounts of 'conscious occurrence'. Lower Mars and Venus should be considered the mounts of 'physical action'. Upper Mars and the Moon are the mounts of 'abstract reaction'.

The Mount of Jupiter

As explained in the first chapter, the Mount of Jupiter represents the 'personal impulse', the area from which our personal, conscious actions arise. It symbolises the soul, the basic governing force in every human being. Traditionally, it is said to be the seat of ambition and pride, representing the principles of birth and expansion, the source of all our physical energy. When well developed it implies that these characteristics are well developed within the personality.

Lines that commence actually upon the Mount of Jupiter are said to be particularly endowed with these qualities. The heart Line is the most likely to rise actually on the Mount of Jupiter, flavouring the emotions with a sense of pride and ambition and adding strength and vehemence to the feelings. The Head Line and the Life Line may be connected to the mount by way of a minor tie line, which will also symbolise an extra flow of these qualities into the habitual patterns of thought, physical energy and the type of lifestyle naturally followed by the subject.

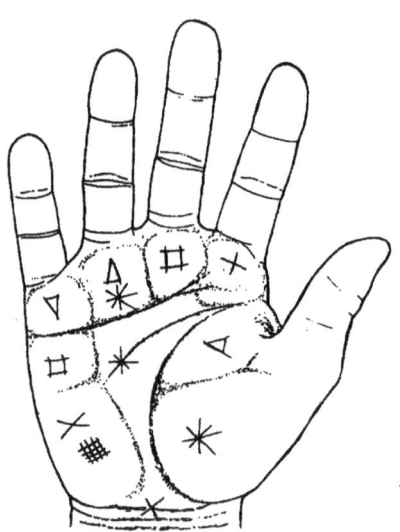

Figure 9

Minor signs: star, cross, triangle, square and grid.

THE MOUNTS

Minor signs or configurations of minor lines may appear on any of the mounts or major lines, and are always regarded as of special significance by the palmist, depending on where they make their appearance. Signs often to be seen on the Mount of Jupiter may be summarised as follows:

Signs on the Mount of Jupiter

Star	High on mount: good fortune; effortless success. Centre mount: pre-eminence in chosen field. Low on mount: never short of influential friends.
Cross	Secure marriage. Social and professional advancement is likely through romantic attachments. Beneath mount: 'The Gambler's Cross'; success with financial arrangements.
Square	Ambitious aims unhindered; any threats to professional integrity easily overcome.
Triangle	Diplomacy. Great ability to organise affairs.
Grid	Selfish, domineering nature.

The Mount of Saturn

Looking at the list of planets within our solar system, we are reminded that Saturn symbolises the principle of time and the limited nature of material life on earth. Mortality, Chronos, Old Father Time, the Grim Reaper — these are all ways of describing the properties of physical life with its inevitability of death, offset with all the benefits of material resources, civilisation, wealth and comfort.

People in whose hand the Mount of Saturn is prominent usually possess a well-developed sense of material values. When the Heart Line rises on this mount rather than on the Mount of

Jupiter, the subject's emotional life will seem well flavoured with practicality, material values, ownership or possessiveness. It is the normal finishing point, too, of the Line of Fate, stressing the material nature of the kind of fate symbolised by this line of 'impersonal influence'.

Minor signs that appear on the Mount of Saturn can carry a warning, and even those with a 'good' connotation sometimes imply a somewhat obsessive interest in the material side of life. A well-marked cross that appears *below* the Mount of Saturn, as a negation of these characteristics, implies an ability to rise above the limitations of mortality, and is known as the 'Mystic Cross'. But a cross actually on this mount is pointing out a strengthening or exaggeration of materiality liable to cause trouble for its wearer.

Signs on the Mount of Saturn

Star	An unwelcome warning of tragic consequences and an ignominious fate through reckless materialism.
Cross	'Sign of the Scaffold'; a stern warning against pursuing material gain to the exclusion of the needs of others.
Square	A seemingly charmed life with regard to finance.
Triangle	Ability to carry out research and analysis.
Grid	Morbid introspection leading to a lack of concentration.

The Mount of the Sun

As a 'planet', or as the god Sol, sometimes identified as Apollo or Helios, patron of poetry and the arts, the Sun represents the cultural centre of the whole person. As the star at the centre of our solar system, all human attributes, both physical and mental, concrete and abstract, revolve around this symbol of wholeness and integrity, prestige, self-worth and fulfilment. A well-developed

Mount of the Sun may be seen in the hand of those who are rich in these qualities, the famous and the highly successful.

The Line of Fortune, one of the lines of 'impersonal influence', is sometimes known as the Sun Line, for it travels from the Rascette at the wrist, the zone of the collective unconscious, to its natural finishing point on this mount. As the recipient of a wedding ring, the 'Sun finger' (for the fingers are often named after their basal mounts) symbolises one who has found the cultural and spiritual completion of marriage — on the physical level, at least. Minor signs that may appear on the Mount of the Sun also carry significance in these areas of human experience, and are listed below.

Signs on the Mount of the Sun

Star	Effortless social attainment. Influential friends.
Cross	High on mount: warning of a loss of prestige. Low on mount: a temporary loss of reputation likely.
Square	Held in high esteem despite occasional setbacks.
Triangle	Ability to handle wealth and fame wisely.
Grid	Tends to attract fame of the wrong sort. Prone to unscrupulous publicity-seeking.

The Mount of Mercury

Beneath the little finger, and last of the mounts of 'conscious occurrence', is the Mount of Mercury. Closest to the Sun, the planet Mercury has been personalised as the messenger of the gods, otherwise known as Hermes; himself the god of learning, science, philosophy, medicine, and business relationships, he represents the power of thought that can bring about civilisation. A well-developed Mount of Mercury expresses the ability to excel in these fields of communication and interaction.

The Mount of Mercury is the natural finishing point of the third line of 'impersonal influence' — the Line of Intuition, carrying messages from the unconscious mind to the awareness of the conscious mind. Depending on the finishing point of the Heart Line, and hence the use to which the emotions are habitually applied, the Mount of Mercury can also indicate the virtue of compassion. Fine lines are sometimes to be seen running downwards from the base of the little finger, and these are known as the 'Marks of Concern', or Medical Stigmata (see chapter 12). Other minor signs to be seen on the Mount of Mercury are summarised below.

Signs on the Mount of Mercury

Star	Welcomes mental challenges. Success in business ventures seems assured.
Cross	Somewhat gullible. Liable to be cheated. Beneath mount: a certain fascination with the occult.
Square	Ability to withstand stress and mental strain.
Triangle	Ability to communicate effortlessly and influence others in business matters.
Grid	A cunning streak. Dishonesty.

The Mount of Venus

The major of the two mounts of 'physical action', Venus represents a person's physical relationships, bodily love and, at the root of sexual relationships and their final outcome, home and family life. Another name for Venus is Aphrodite, goddess of beauty and sensual love, and mother of Cupid. A well-developed Mount of Venus denotes a person in whom sensual awareness is strongly developed and particularly important. This mount comprises the muscular area at the base of the thumb, delineated by the Life Line.

THE MOUNTS

It is often criss-crossed by minor lines, and these carry significance for the palmist.

Concentric lines running more or less parallel with the Life Line, curving around the mount, are said to represent others for whom the subject has felt passionate devotion. Probably they never were connected with the idea of marriage, but each of these lines will enshrine the happy memories of a past romance — or perhaps a romance yet to come. Lines radiating from the base of the thumb and running outwards towards the Life Line also represent romantic liaisons, and in this case they are of a more permanent and ongoing nature. They do not necessarily imply marriage, but they have affected or will affect the whole outcome of family life. Other signs to be found on the Mount of Venus are as follows.

Signs on the Mount of Venus

Star	High on mount: 'The Rising Star of Venus'; romantic happiness. Low on mount: 'The Setting Star of Venus'; close ties with home and family precluding romantic attachments.
Cross	Faithfulness in marriage, with a single lover.
Square	Well protected against the possibility of broken romances.
Triangle	Jealousy. Tendency to manipulate family and marriage partners.
Grid	Romantic success seems unlikely. Obstacles always seem to appear, hindering the course of true love.

The Lower Mount of Mars

Above the Mount of Venus, and formed largely by the gripping muscles of the hand when folded into a fist, the Lower Mount of

Mars is the second mount of 'physical action', based on the principle of action through the function of bodily sensation. Its chief characteristic is aggression, and it follows that people in whose hand this mount is particularly well developed tend to possess a confrontational nature. A poorly developed mount indicates a retiring, non-aggressive nature. This is not to say that all retiring or quiet-natured people are non-aggressive; indeed, shy people are often very aggressive, and will be very likely to possess a prominent mount below a high-arching Life Line that is well joined to the Head Line. These features will be made clear later on in the book.

In the case of people who are courageous rather than confrontational, the Life Line will usually rise on, rather than above, this mount, or it will certainly be connected to it by means of minor tie-lines. When the Head Line itself rises on the Lower Mount of Mars, however, cutting through the Life Line, you can be sure that this is the hand of a bad-tempered person, quick to express rage. Signs that may appear on the Lower Mount of Mars are summarised below.

Signs on the Lower Mount of Mars

Star	A stern warning against the use of violence. An aggressive nature.
Cross	Again a stern warning. This sign often portends a violent end brought about by an aggressive attitude. Adjacent to the mount on the 'Plain of Mars': bad temper.
Square	A seemingly charmed life in dangerous circumstances. Attracted by high-risk occupations.
Triangle	Courageous, Ability to keep a cool head in difficult circumstances.
Grid	A habitual trouble-seeker.

THE MOUNTS

The Mount of the Moon

Having examined the side of the hand expressing objectivity, we move from action to reaction and examine the two remaining mounts based on the subjective side of the hand. First and most important is the Mount of the Moon, the large fleshy area opposite the Mount of Venus. When this mount is particularly well developed, it implies ownership of a creative imagination. The closer to the wrist, the more 'unconscious', the more intuitive is its implied nature. When the lower regions of this mount are prominent and fleshy, so as to overhang the topmost bracelet of the Rascette, the palmist can be sure that the hand belongs to an intuitive person to whom the realms of the paranormal are all-important.

Where the Mount of Venus is connected with home and family, tradition has it that its counterpart, the Mount of the Moon, is connected with outsiders, with travel abroad, and with the influence of non-family members. Special signs on the Mount of the Moon may be interpreted according to the summary below.

Signs on the Mount of the Moon

Star	Indiscretion. Prone to taking unnecessary risks. Warning to take special care when travelling.
Cross	Liable to exaggerate. Fond of grandiose schemes. Indiscrete tendency to enter 'where wise men fear to tread'.
Square	Ability to endure apparent hardships, especially when travelling.
Triangle	Ability to succeed in artistic and literary work.
Grid	Nervous tension.

The Upper Mount of Mars

The two Martian mounts together symbolise the passions, the determination, the obstinacy, the will-power, the grit, of people who get things done in the world. In the objective, physical field these characteristics take on the appearance of aggression. In the subjective, abstract side of the personality, they take on the intangible quality of tenacity, the application of stamina and dedication. These latter qualities are expressed in the hand by the Upper Mount of Mars. When this mount is particularly well developed, the subject is likely to possess above-average staying power. In common with the Mount of the Moon, the Upper Mount of Mars is a frequent ending point of the Head Line, and sometimes the Heart Line too, symbolising the ability of the heart and the mind to stay on course and persevere against all odds. Minor signs on this mount may be interpreted as follows.

Signs on the Upper Mount of Mars

Star	Quarrelsome. Stubborn.
Cross	A warning against the risk of physical injury brought about by stubbornness.
Square	Tremendous energy and stamina. Able to keep going without coming to harm. Forthright but good-tempered.
Triangle	Ability to organise effective resistance against oppression or exploitation. A tireless care-worker.
Grid	Bad temper.

3
CHEIROGNOMY; HANDS, FINGERS AND THUMBS

The cheirotype

The cheirotype sums up the general appearance and proportions of the hand, and classifies its owner into one or other of five basic personality types. With a little practice a person's cheirotype will be obvious at first glance, but there is a set of simple measurements which will help you to assess a personality type more accurately:

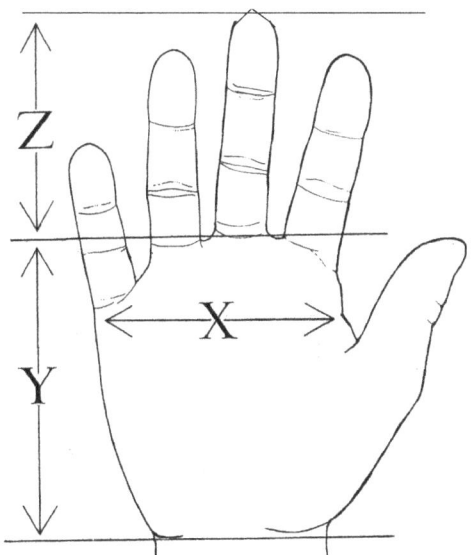

Figure 10

Measurements for finding the cheirotype

Two factors are involved in obtaining these measurements: the percentage by which the width of the palm is greater or lesser than its length, a factor which we call P; and the percentage by which the fingers are longer or shorter than the width of the palm, a factor which we call F. The diagram gives the required measurements as X, Y and Z. The unit of measurement you choose to use, whether inches or centimetres, is irrelevant, provided of course the same method is used throughout. The simple equations which need to be calculated are as follows:

$$P = \frac{X}{X+Y} \times 100 \qquad F = \frac{Z}{Z+X} \times 100$$

CHEIROTYPE	'Rugged' AA	'Practical' A	'Normal' O	'Artistic' B	'Sensitive' BB
P factor F factor	More than 48 Less than 45	48–46 45–48	46–45 49–50	45–44 51–52	43 or less 53 or more
Compatible fingertips	Square	Blunt	Rounded	Conical	Pointed

The 'Normal' classification describes the average hand, with fingers about equal in length to the width of the palm. Most people's fingertips as a rule are rounded. On each side of the 'Normal' hand (O) are two very common variations: the 'Practical' (A), and the 'Artistic' (B). On either side of these again are two more extreme types: the 'Rugged' (AA), and the 'Sensitive' (BB). At the one extreme the AA hand is short and thick, with square-tipped fingers. At the other extreme the BB type is long and delicate, with finely pointed, slender fingers. Most of the diagrams in this book show Rounded (O) fingertips.

Spatulate fingertips are quite often to be seen within the central range of cheirotypes. Sometimes, the effect is produced by habitual work which entails pressing down with the fingers, but

CHEIROGNOMY: HANDS, FINGERS AND THUMBS

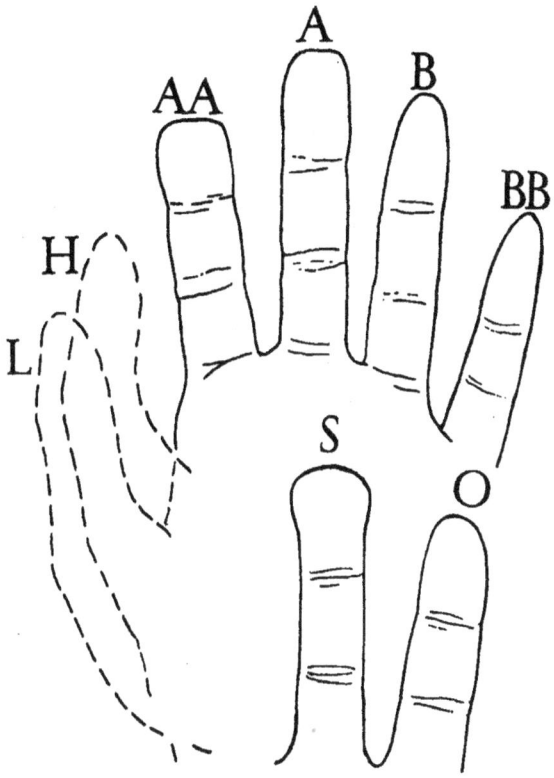

Figure 11
 Fingertips: (AA) square; (A) blunt; (B) conical; (BB) pointed;
 (O) rounded; (S) spatulate
 Thumbs: (H) high-set; (L) low-set.

more often it is an inherited characteristic. The soft underside of the topmost phalange has a distinctly bulbous, swelling outline, and it is often possessed by people who produce beautiful things, or in the case of musicians, beautiful sounds, with their hands. It seems to add a mildly eccentric and sometimes obsessive dimension to the cheirotype.

The names of these five cheirotypes reflect their personalities fairly precisely. The normal or average person is just that, a basic all-rounder, reasonably practical, reasonably artistic, a person without extreme characteristics in either direction. Practical types may have had their hands modified by hard work, but by nature they will probably be hard-working, sensible and reliable, usually quite content to follow routine and accept the conventional attitudes of their contemporaries. The artistic type will probably tend more towards the principle of personal choice and freedom in matters of lifestyle and morality. His or her life will probably be found to follow a more adventurous and individualistic course than that of the practical person, and security or conventional rules will not seem so important an issue.

The two extreme types seem to have carried these differences of attitude and approach much further. The 'Rugged' type of personality may sometimes seem to be lacking in all the finer and more subtle characteristics that are admired in the worlds of fashion and etiquette. He or she may seem coarse and unfeeling, exactly the opposite of the 'Sensitive' type, who is likely to be ultra-refined, with intensely developed feelings. At the one extreme a spade cannot be other than a spade, and abstract considerations may seem to be lacking. At the other extreme practical considerations may scarcely seem to enter the awareness; the abstract idea, and the feeling it produces, are the things that matter.

In some hands the cheirotype may seem to be mixed. A practical hand with delicate fingertips may belong to a craftsperson who produces delicate and beautiful artefacts. An artistic hand with blunt fingertips may be the badge of one whose creative talents are put to use in unusually solid, tactile ways, quite possibly but not necessarily a sculptor, or more likely a producer, a manufacturer, a director or publisher, one well able to put creative talents to profitable use.

Size and general appearance of the hand also have significance in assessing character. Typically, large hands belong to quiet, phlegmatic people, those who think a lot and speak their thoughts slowly and carefully. Small hands tend to belong to more forthright characters, people who think quickly and speak out readily. A bossy person almost invariably has small hands. The case is similar as regards the size and prominence of the knuckle joints. Quiet, stolid, somewhat introverted people tend to possess gnarled or knotty knuckles. Extroverts of the impulsive type are more likely to have smooth fingers and knuckle joints.

Fingers

Comparative length of fingers has significance within the cheirotype, besides the general tendency for fingers to be short, as with an 'AA', or long, as with a 'BB' type. Take the first finger — the index, or Jupiter finger, and compare its length with that of the third — the Sun finger. When these two fingers are of more or less the same length, we can assume that the subject is a well-balanced person who gets on well with others. The longer the index finger seems in relation to the third finger, the more domineering and ambitious the person is likely to be. Pride and an unspoken sense of superiority will be inbuilt. The shorter the index finger when compared with the third finger, the more will the opposite apply. The possessor of a very short index finger is likely to be excessively cautious, and may well suffer from feelings of inferiority. These are the two extremes, and the hand will usually reveal a tendency in one direction or the other, to be interpreted in the light of all the remaining information available. There are medical implications too, relating to fertility: a man whose Sun finger is longer than the index finger is likely to have a higher level of testosterone than usual; a woman whose index finger is longer than her Sun finger, is likely to have a high level of oestrogen.

If the Jovian characteristics of the index finger are related to ambition, the nature of Saturn, interpreted by way of the second finger, relates to the Saturnian type of personality, and to the habitual ways in which we cope with the limitations of material resources, and our place in the environment. When this second or middle finger is particularly long and seemingly well developed, it suggests a person well able to cope with a modicum of hardship and, indeed, one to whom a certain amount of hardship is sure to

THE ART OF PALMISTRY

come. It is said that we all have our own small cross to bear. Some people have great self-discipline, and are quite likely to be found living, perhaps on their own, under difficult conditions. They are usually serious, thoughtful and philosophical people, the exact opposite of one in whose hand the second finger is scarcely longer than its neighbours. Such a person will have very little patience with lone hardship, and is unlikely to be found pulling a sledge across Antarctic wastes. He or she will naturally gravitate to wherever life seems to present the least trouble, the fewest problems.

The third or Sun finger is next in line, We have already noted that when this finger and the index finger are evenly balanced, the owner's character will be equally evenly balanced and normally self-confident. When the first and second fingers are

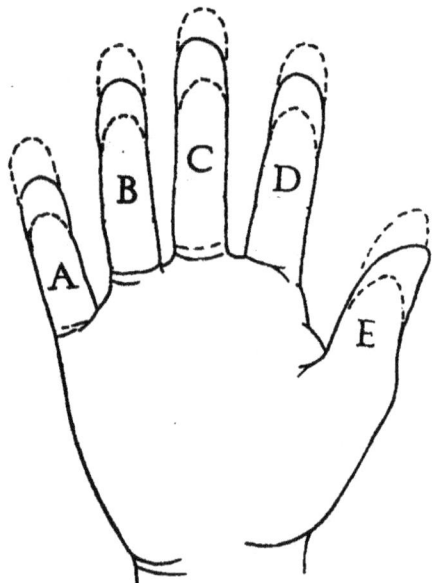

Figure 12
Comparative length of fingers. (A)long: talkative; (A)short: reserved.
(B)long: seeking public acclaim; (B)short: retiring nature.
(C)long: self-disciplined; (C)short: indulgent nature.
(D)long: ambitious; (D)short: cautious nature.
(E)long: dominating; (E)short: submissive.

in proportion, but the Sun finger is particularly long and well developed, all the ambition indicated by the index finger will be directed along the path of abstract rather than material fortune — towards the principles of prestige and good publicity. This is particularly the case when the lowest phalange of the Sun finger appears noticeably longer than the two above it.

Finally the little, or Mercury finger, may be considered for length and comparative appearance. It should reach more or less to the top joint, or the base of the first phalange, of the Sun finger, to be considered of average length. Mercurian characteristics are connected with the principle of communication. An unusually long little finger implies that its owner may seem unable to stop talking for very long. Good actors and impressionists in particular are likely to display this characteristic; it can be a great asset when their calling or situation in life demands the gift of loquacity, but they can be a trial to everybody around them when it does not. It is the finger most closely connected with skill in business too, and a lack of business ability is displayed when the little finger is unusually short.

Phalanges

Significance when the phalanges are noticeably long

Digit	Top	Middle	Lower
Jupiter (1st finger)	Ambition pursued for intellectual satisfaction	Ambition pursued for emotional satisfaction	Ambition pursued for physical satisfaction
Saturn (2nd finger)	Given to factual analysis	Fondness for the natural world	Acquisitive nature
Sun (3rd finger)	Broad cultural interests	Love of art or music	Practical expertise in art or music
Mercury (4th finger)	Inventive in communication	Guarded in communication	Brashness of display

Significance of phalange length in the thumb

Top	Lower
Long: strong-willed to the point of stubbornness	Long: thoughtful and discreet
Short: easily swayed	Short: reckless

Comparative length of the phalanges is given significance depending upon the traditional symbolism of each finger, and these significances are listed here. You will notice that the topmost phalange in each case relates to the intellectual or rational application of the quality represented by its own particular finger. The middle phalange reflects the emotional application, or value-judgement, of that quality. The lower phalange relates to the practical or physical application of that quality. A long phalange expresses comparative exaggeration of a characteristic; a short phalange expresses shortage within this facet of the psyche.

Curves

A finger which shows a natural curve can tell you something about its owner. Flexibility, or lack of it, can give the fingers the appearance of a curve, either forwards towards the palm when rather stiff and inflexible, or backwards when flexible. A forwards curve is said to imply a somewhat grasping nature, and it certainly demonstrates a certain inflexibility of character. It typifies a stickler for rules and regulations, one with a prudent and strictly practical nature. A backwards curve shows flexibility of character, with little regard for rules or conventions. Backwards-curving fingers usually belong to interesting, entertaining people, but they often seem to have a poor sense of business and financial management.

The diagram opposite shows the sideways type of curve: the index finger sometimes shows a distinct curve towards its neighbouring fingers. This indicates great determination and will-power, with an element of stubbornness, the sign of an achiever. The implication is that the Jovian personal impulse, the basic driving force, is being strengthened by the Saturnian force of materiality: ambitions brought to reality.

The third, Sun, finger often shows a bias towards the Saturnian member, implying a leaning towards the best use of material resources with regard to the principle of wholeness: that is, time and money will be spent on the aims of personal fulfilment and prestige, the feel-good factor. For the possessor of an inwards-curving Sun finger, an unspoken question surrounds many day-to-day decisions regarding what is to be done for the best. When pronounced, the trait can indicate a touch of neurotic anxiety or a defensive attitude, all connected with the idea of self worth. And of course, such questions are well justified for the person concerned. We do need to act for the best in the long run, and if we are to get on in the world, it does matter what other people think of us.

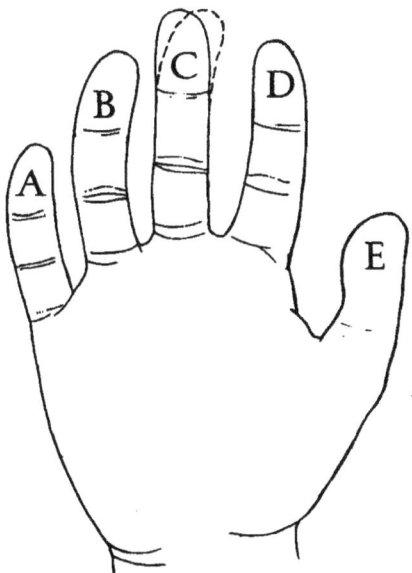

Figure 13
Curvature of the fingers: (A) shrewdness; (B) awareness of the need for a good reputation; (C) use of resources to further ambition; (D) strong will-power; (E) 'pugilist's thumb'.

Finally, there may be a bias of the little finger, the Mercurial finger of communication, towards the cultural sphere of the Sun and, in the same direction, towards the material, resourceful and ambitious fields of the remaining two fingers. The possessor of an inwards-curving little finger will certainly show a good head for business, and a shrewd capacity for devising money-making schemes. He or she will also be diplomatic and tactful, an expert mediator when disagreements are in the air.

There is another curve associated with the fingers — the curve of the set or alignment. In the great majority of hands the Saturnian finger is set higher, or further forward than the others, so that the four fingers are aligned on a curve. In cases where this normal characteristic is exaggerated and the curve is more pronounced than usual, the implication is that life is fated to be more of a struggle than average for the person concerned. A markedly low-set Jupiter finger will imply a shortage of the Jovian qualities of self-confidence and self-assertion. A low-set little finger will imply a shortage of the Mercurial characteristics of communication, social and business skills. This is an unfortunate but quite common circumstance. Success, as a rule, does not come easily to any person with this feature in their hand, unless it is compensated for by other factors.

The opposite applies when the base of the fingers shows a more or less even set, as near as possible to a straight line. The fingers will then appear more equal in length than average. A straight set of fingers and worldly success seem to go hand in glove, though a completely straight alignment is rarely to be seen. Top politicians and people in high public places, however, almost invariably possess a straighter than average set of fingers.

Finger span

When someone lays their hand flat on a table top, in a way that is relaxed and unselfconscious, you may notice that the method of doing this differs from person to person. Some individuals spread their fingers wide, others hold them tightly together. In many cases

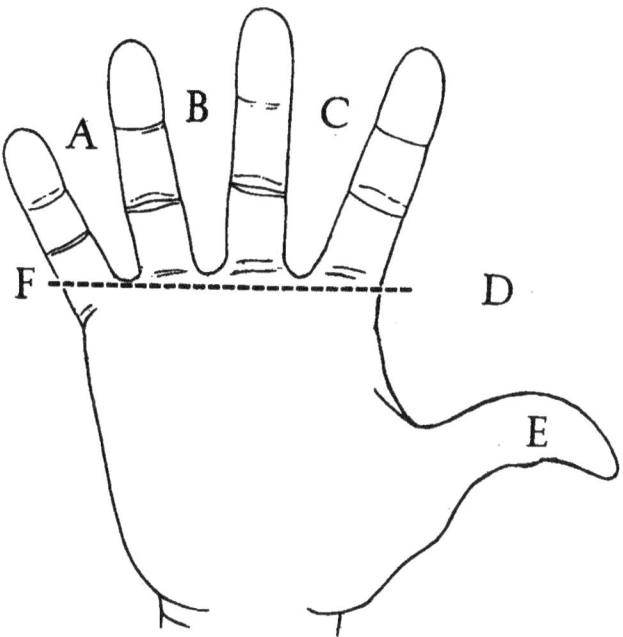

Figure 14

Finger span. A comparatively wide spread shows: (A) a dislike of convention; (B) an easy-going, relaxed personality; (C) self-confidence and determination; (D) generosity and sympathy; (E) flexible thumb shows a flexible nature; (F) even alignment at the base of the fingers indicates a high achiever.

there will be a pronounced gap between two fingers in particular — let us say the little finger and the Sun finger — whilst the others are held comparatively close to each other. The palmist can read significance into this.

Fingers that are all spread fairly widely when relaxed in this fashion tend to belong to frank and open people; those who would probably feel they have nothing to hide, people who can face the future without apprehension. When the opposite is the case, and the fingers are held stiffly together, we can be sure that their owner is excessively cautious, not very sociable, and probably given to worrying constantly about what the future may bring.

When a pronounced gap is left between the little Mercury finger and its neighbouring Sun finger, the person concerned will prove to be an independent type who dislikes rigid rules and conventions. He or she will probably be full of original ideas, and will feel the need to communicate them in a friendly manner. A wide gap between the second, Saturnian finger and the third, Sun finger, implies that the principle of limitation and discipline as typified by Saturn is not allowed to infringe upon the Sun principle of cultural expectations and social status. This person will be easy-going, if not devil-may-care, and will seem to care nothing at all about saving for a rainy day. You will not find them fretting about what fate may have in store. When the most pronounced gap appears between the first, Jupiter finger, and the Saturn finger, the subject is likely to maintain a distance between these two principles in real life. The driving power of Jupiter — personal ambition, the fulfilment of his or her own idea of what is fitting — is not allowed to be thwarted by outside considerations. This is the sign of a forceful personality who is not really interested in what others may think or feel.

Finally, the relaxed hand may show a particularly wide gap between the first finger and the thumb. This is really a sign of the best and most civilised, the most 'human' of qualities. Such a person is likely to be generous and outgoing, always sympathetic and ready to lend a hand or do a favour.

Thumbs

The interpretation given to a generous gap between thumb and first finger is the same as when the thumb is low-set, that is, when it springs from the hand comparatively low down, near the wrist. The set of the thumb is shown on page 37. A low-set thumb indicates a character we can all admire: humane, courageous, and thoroughly civilised.

A high-set thumb, by contrast, is said to indicate a somewhat tight-fisted attitude, both to money and to information or conversation. Of course, this may be offset by other factors, and by the exercise of free will. A high-set thumb does not automatically condemn you to meanness, but it might be worthwhile looking for the trait in yourself just in case.

Length of thumb and its phalanges

Length of thumb has significance chiefly in the fields of dominance, will-power, and the application of logic as opposed to feeling. A long-thumbed person will tend to be domineering; if taken to extremes, even tyrannical. So strong-willed a person may seem charming and courteous and display charisma, but he or she may prove quite ruthless in cases where a short-thumbed person would be inclined to compromise. The long thumbs of the world, therefore, tend to get their own way.

Short-thumbed people lack tenacity. Though they may well be argumentative, their arguments will veer from tack to tack, and they are readily swayed by the tones of emotion. Far from being dominant in social situations, such people will be submissive to such an extent that they allow themselves to be overruled and elbowed out.

Comparative length of the two phalanges of the thumb also has significance in cheirognomy. In this context the thumb expresses the ability to grip and hold in an abstract sense, involving both will and forethought. The topmost phalange will indicate whether its wearer is difficult or easy to budge from any preconception he or she may hold. When this phalange is noticeably longer than the lower one, we have an extremely stubborn personality. The lower phalange of the thumb expresses the virtue of discretion, or its lack. A noticeably long lower phalange is likely to be owned by one who will ponder long and hard before taking action.

Flexibility

Thumbs within the range of average length will be found to vary in flexibility. Noticeably flexible thumbs which bend themselves slightly backwards when relaxed indicate a flexible, adaptable character who tends not to have firm opinions. Supple thumbs tend to belong to those who dislike rules and conventions, and tend to be tolerant of shortcomings, both in others and in themselves. They also tend to lack firmness of purpose, however, and are butterflies when circumstances call for prolonged concentration.

Stiff-thumbed people tend to be stiff and unbending themselves in their views and their sense of right and wrong. They may be adventurous physically and mentally, but cautious in their emotions. They are unlikely to allow their feelings to run away with them. They are the most reliable of people, as a rule, and stick by their principles and their word long after a flexible-thumbed person will have forgotten all about the matter.

A stiff thumb combined with a full, fleshy underside to the topmost phalange, giving it the profile of a club, is the badge of an aggressive, short-tempered person. It is sometimes called the 'pugilist's thumb' (see page 43), though its owner may appear friendly and civilised until they happen to lose their temper. When this happens it is advisable to duck or run for cover; their arguments can quickly become physical.

Waist size

There are two more distinctive thumb types which can give a clue to personality: the thick and the thin-waisted thumbs. The former, when seen from the knuckle side, is more or less the same thickness from top to bottom. The latter narrows below the central joint, giving it the distinctive thin-waisted appearance. The difference is largely a matter of diplomacy. The person with a thin-waisted thumb will always use tact when dealing with others, even to the point of never quite saying what they mean. The thick-waisted thumb belongs to the person who takes pride in saying 'I believe in speaking my mind!'. Tact is not a virtue in their ears, they believe in calling a spade a spade.

Bulk

Apart from length, outline and flexibility, there is the simple overall factor of comparative size or bulk. At first glance, one person's thumbs may appear heavy or large in proportion to the rest of their hand; another person's thumbs may appear to be comparatively slight. It will usually be found that the slight-thumbed person is one who always wants to be taken seriously. His or her pronouncements are intended to be factual and constructive, typical perhaps of the politicians and spokespersons of the world. The heavy-thumbed person projects the opposite impression: he or she *wants* to be taken with a pinch of salt. Such people may make public pronouncements, but there is always a twinkle in the eye, a tongue in the cheek. Heavy thumbs tend to belong to the raconteurs, the stand-up comics, the dedicated jokers of the world.

Fingerprints

In chapter one it was mentioned that identical twins possess very similar patterns of lines on their palms. No such similarity is to be seen with regard to their fingerprints, however; they are no more likely to prove identical than they would be with any two people randomly compared. This fact gives a clue as to the nature and extent of personality variation to be deduced from the fingerprints. The differences are subtle, such as would perhaps be well known to close friends and relatives, but not so obvious to others. Nevertheless, they are real enough to record quite reliably matters of attitude, or sensitivity, of nervous energy, of susceptibility to stress and worry, and therefore, to a large extent, of health.

Despite the millions of pattern variations that exist, finger or thumb prints can be divided into just five basic types: the whorl, the loop, the high arch, the low arch, and the composite (see overleaf). In the case of many people, each of their fingertips bears the same type of print. In the case of many others, however, some fingers may have one print, some another. Using our knowledge of the mounts and the particular facet of the personality which they and their fingers represent, we can deduce how these subtle characteristics are likely to make their effect known in each individual. The little finger, for instance, as the representative of communication and business skills, may be whorled — the 'high-powered' print; the third finger, representing matters of culture and self-esteem, may bear a looped print to indicate more easy-going characteristics in this psychological department.

The whorled pattern is the most forceful and dedicated of the fingerprint types. The person with ten whorled fingertips will be a high-flyer, but may suffer from stress. As this is the sign of an independent and somewhat dogmatic nature, the whorl can be seen as the symbol of intensity in the fields of ambition, pride, material resources, money-making, business dealings and communication, and leisure activities too, when it appears on the Jupiter, Saturn and Mercury fingers. A whorled Sun finger in addition belongs to the kind of person who tends to blame himself or herself for any lack of perfection, and this trait adds greatly to psychological stress, affecting the physical action of the heart.

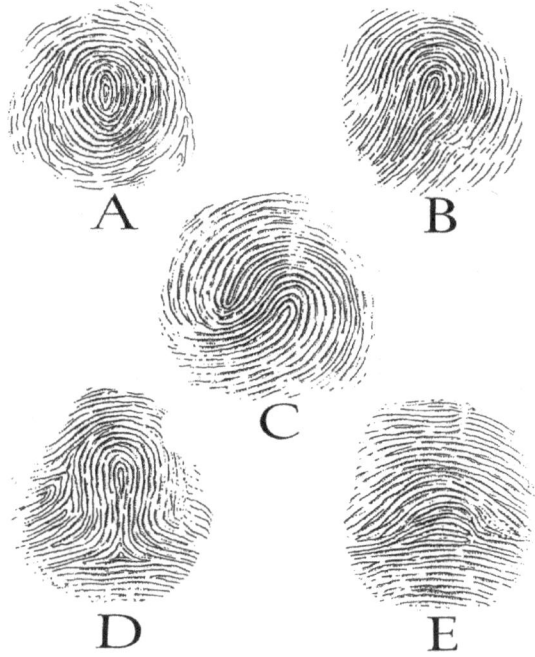

Figure 15
Fingerprints: (A) whorl; (B) loop; (C) composite; (D) high arch; (E) low arch.

The loop fingerprint belongs to one who is adaptable and versatile, typical of the Mercurial type, possessing a quick mind and readily expressed emotional responses. He or she will be more easy-going than the whorled fingerprinter, but still clearly focused and highly independent. Success or failure will not be so vitally important an issue, however, as the loop fingerprinter always feels able to switch tracks and pursue some alternative course when things become too stressful.

The composite fingerprint has the appearance of a double loop, almost as though each were trying to cancel out the other, and this element of contradiction is reflected in its wearer's personality. Indecision is always to the forefront of the composite fingerprinter's life, and as it seems so difficult for them to stick to any particular course, idea or principle, they often appear unreliable. There is seldom any intent to deceive, however; they tend to set out in one direction, only to find themselves diverted along completely opposing lines, to the bafflement of their colleagues.

The high arch print represents a character similar in some ways to the loop, in other ways to the whorl fingerprinter. He or she will have a quick and responsive mind, will be intensely focused, and will be likely to suffer from stress at times. Often highly strung and emotionally sensitive, high arch printers often show great talent for music and the arts.

The low arch fingerprinter is unlikely to suffer from an excess of sensitivity, and tends to be materialistic in his or her approach to the finer things of life. Emotional responses will be guarded, and they dislike letting their true feelings be known. They tend to be sceptical in the extreme, and seldom accept anything on face value alone. These characteristics fit them admirably for investigative work where cold facts must not be obscured by sentiment.

The full picture

Never be dogmatic when reading the hand. Always remember that you are assembling a mind-picture of the whole person, and people are far more than the mere sum of their various parts. You may be assessing the fingerprints, the general cheirotype, or the individual lines and signs of a hand, but none of these can be taken as cut-and-dried indications of a person's character. Every small hint that you gain from a study of the hand goes towards building up a portrait of the whole person, and all these minor factors will become modified as that portrait takes shape. Remember you are creating something that should be of value and interest to your subject, and this means that your diagnoses should be as positive, constructive, and flexible as possible.

Left and right hands

Throughout this book we shall be looking at the subtle differences between the left and the right hands. These differences can only be appreciated fully once the basics of palmistry have been understood, so we shall have to wait until chapter fifteen for a full discussion.

'Intelligent, understanding, sincere, generous, imaginative but sensible ... Yes, that's *very* accurate.'

4

THE HEART LINE

The flow of feelings

The nature and intensity of a person's emotional feelings may be assessed very readily by a glance at their Heart Line. The quality and strength or insistence of emotion does vary greatly from person to person: in some people it is stronger by far than their power of rational thought; in others it seems little more than an extra faculty that can be called upon when fine value-judgements are required. In palmistry, powerful emotions are suggested by a full-length, deeply etched Heart Line; weak emotions are suggested when this line is short and only faintly delineated. The fainter the line, the less vehement the expression of feelings. A particularly retiring person who does not care for confrontation, and who tends to hide his or her true feelings, may possess a long Heart Line, but it is likely to be fairly faint.

In the case of a deeply etched Heart Line, we can be sure that emotions play an important part in that person's daily life, and the nature of those feelings will be expressed by the curvature of the line. A markedly straight Heart Line will suggest a discreet and emotionally stable person. Emotions in this case may be powerfully felt inwardly, but they will not find vehement expression: they will be expressed in a calm and calculated manner. Hurt feelings will make themselves known through barbs of sarcasm rather than through violent emotional tussle.

A Heart Line that is short, straight and deeply delineated often turns out to belong to a violently emotional person, prone to fiercely passionate struggles during the course of which loving tenderness will seem to have been forgotten amid floods of tears and flung ashtrays. Love-hate relationships are to be expected here,

THE ART OF PALMISTRY

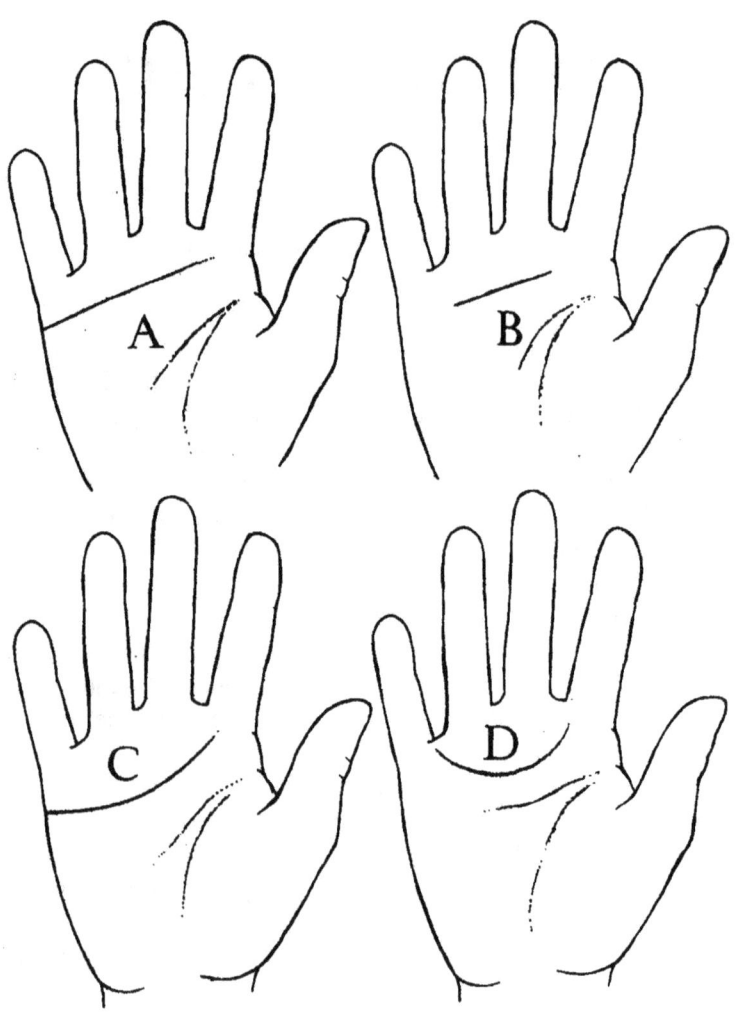

Figure 16
The Heart Line: (A) long and straight; (B) short and straight; (C) long and curved; (D) short and curved.

THE HEART LINE

for hate is certainly a branch of passion, the intensity of feeling that is expressed in the hand by the Heart Line. Straightness implies uncompromising directness of emotional expression. A curve in the Heart Line suggests a willingness to bend emotionally, to accommodate another's moods.

In general, the more closely the Heart Line runs to the mounts at the base of the fingers, the more closely will the emotions be held in check. The further away from the mounts the line ventures, the more scope they are given for uncontrolled expression. A long and deeply curving Heart Line (figure 16C) is likely to be seen in the hand of a temperamental but often deeply affectionate person. Discretion is not likely to be the strong point of this character, and when a love affair is in progress, as it usually will be, there is no secret about it. Compassionate devotion is the saving grace expressed by the deeply curving Heart Line, for the emotions, like the line, will be powerful and flow very deeply. When things go wrong, however, and the love affair turns sour, there will be inevitable emotional upheavals. Such a person will certainly seem to be 'all heart'; they 'wear their heart on their sleeve'.

The Mount of Mercury is the seat of compassion, the result of sympathetic communication, and this fine quality is most likely to be expressed in cases where the Heart Line curves around this mount at the base of the little finger, as though embracing it. A Heart Line that is short and markedly curved (figure 16D), so that it stops short of the Mount of Mercury and, instead, curves around the Mount of the Sun, belongs to a person who is not in the habit of expressing his or her feelings openly. Such people will feel deeply, though their companions and partners may not realise how much they are taking things to heart because their exterior remains unruffled. They are simply not communicating their feelings. Instead, they are embracing, through their feelings, everything that goes to make up the hidden qualities of an individual, their 'inner culture'. They will not be 'hiding' their feelings: they simply will not care too greatly about what others may think or feel. Their emotional aim in life is to fortify their own sense of self-worth, to make themselves a 'better person' in their own judgement. They will probably be entirely affectionate and amiable, but red-hot passion is not for them, and they may well acquire a name for 'living in a world of their own'.

The rising point

Referring back to chapter 1, you will see that the *rising point* of the Heart Line is of great significance. Its natural source could be said to be the Mount of Jupiter, the symbolic seat of all personal impulses. In practice, however, its rising point is usually shared to some extent with the Mount of Saturn, symbolic seat of everything that *limits* the unopposed libido. Think of the Heart Line as a river flowing across the plain of the palm, rising on the high ground of the mounts and the head of the valley between them. Rivers usually have tributaries, and when they do, they can be said to have risen in more than one place.

A Heart Line that rises without tributaries on the Mount of Jupiter (figure 17A), will carry the undiluted nature of that mount along the course of that subject's emotional life. Ambition and pride will both be powerful features in that life, and will flavour the expression of feelings. That person's marriage and relationships will be based upon ambition, on improvement, and this will certainly result in a well-considered match likely to lead on to better things. But such a match will not necessarily be permanent, for perfection is an elusive quarry. Pride, however, will ensure that any partnership will be well thought of by outsiders, and not seem to be lacking, either in material means or in propriety or moral justification. In practical terms, a marriage spouse with a Jupiter-risen Heart Line will wish whole-heartedly to be faithful, and will defend that partnership vigorously when it needs defending. And should fate decree that the arrangement proves, after all, not to be permanent, that basic certainty of purpose will still apply as strongly as ever: the inevitable changeover will be accompanied by much emotional anguish.

Now suppose that the river of emotional feelings, expressed by the Heart Line, rises on the Mount of Saturn (figure 17B), again without tributaries. The emotions in this case will have

THE HEART LINE

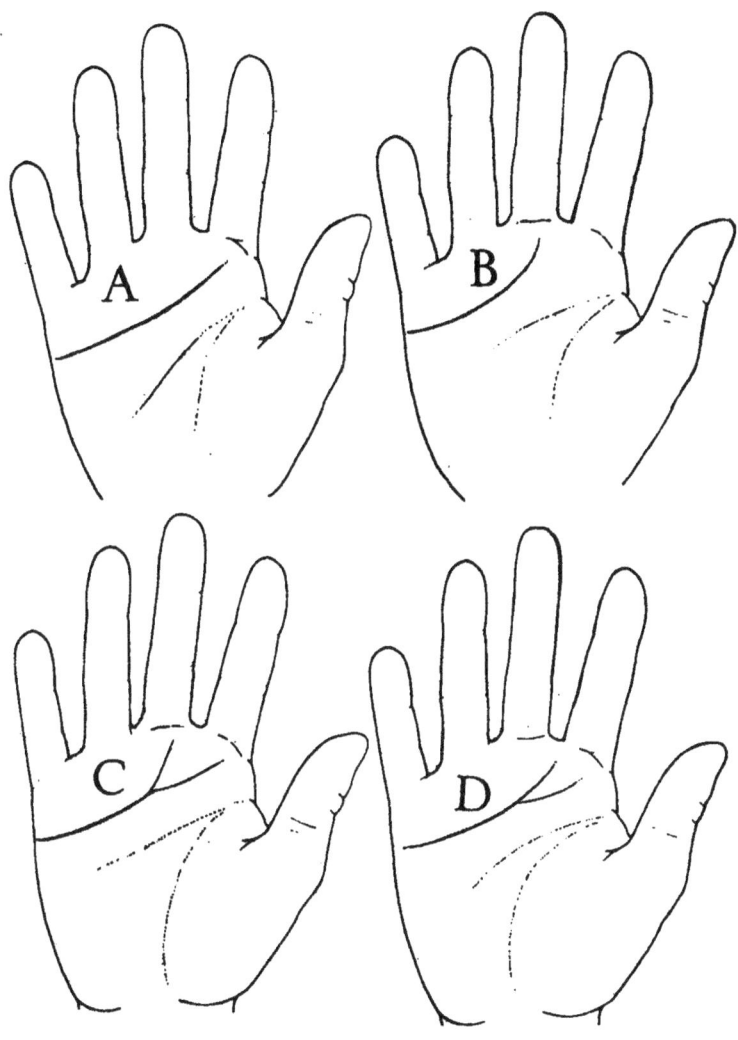

Figure 17
The Heart Line: (A) rising on the Mount of Jupiter; (B) rising on the Mount of Saturn; (C) with tributaries from both mounts; (D) with tributaries from the Mount of Jupiter and between the mounts.

a completely different flavour, for they will be occupied chiefly with materiality. Material resources will be the main emotional concern, and the principle of gain will be the driving force. The person with this uncompromising Heart Line will not seem to be short of 'pride', but pride of this sort is merely another name for 'ownership'. He or she will probably make a good marriage, for the choice of partner will certainly be the best available. Family and friends will be well looked after, for ownership implies responsibility, and the person with a Saturn-risen Heart Line feels emotionally that those who are to some extent dependent, are to that extent owned. Dedicated bigamists fall naturally into this category. When normal marriage partnerships involving people of this emotional type run into trouble, unpleasant litigation and financial demands may well ensue. This person will care for everything and everybody, providing the object of their care can be 'owned', and they will do so quite lavishly if they have the means. However, no regard whatsoever will be paid to outsiders, to the feelings of people who are not 'owned' in this way, and the rules of society will apply only when it pays to follow them. As always, however, this feature must be interpreted in the context of the hands as a whole, and of individual free will.

These are the two extremes: the Jupiter and the Saturn Heart Liners. Fortunately, perhaps, the majority of people have tributaries to their Heart Line, so that in practice such extremes are modified and diluted. The presence of tributaries implies that the course of emotional life is seldom clear and unequivocal; there will be choices and changes of heart. When tributaries to the Heart Line rise equally upon the two mounts (figure 17C), the subject will still seem somewhat extreme in his or her emotional life, but their actions and attitudes will not be fixed. They are liable to chop and change between the attitudes of the two 'planets': sometimes Jovian, proud but light-hearted; sometimes Saturnian, stern and materialistic.

If the mounts, as rising points of the Heart Line, suggest basic emotional priorities that are fixed, so the valleys or areas between the mounts denote flexibility and impartiality. Compromise is always a possibility for the person whose Heart

THE HEART LINE

Line rises between the Mounts of Jupiter and Saturn; his or her emotional life will be coloured by both extremes, without being governed by either. Tributaries in any case imply a softening of the basic viewpoint, even when they all arise from one mount or the other. A totally Jupiter-risen Heart Line with two or three tributaries on that mount, or a totally Saturn-risen one with two or three tributaries, are to that extent an improvement on a single rising.

If you are looking for indications of whether a marriage will be happy or not, all tributaries to the Heart Line are a good omen. They indicate a subtle broadening of the feelings, an ability to see the other's point of view, a willingness to give and take, upon which all happy relationships depend.

It is mainly a matter of degree. One person's hand may have two tributaries to the Heart Line, one from the Mount of Jupiter and one from between the mounts; another may have a tributary rising from between the mounts, another from the Mount of Saturn. These people may be orientated respectively towards the principle of Jupiter, with its drive towards the abstract goal of personal fulfilment, or towards the principle of Saturn, with its more tangible interest in the acquisition of worldly things; but in either case they will understand and have respect for the opposite viewpoint; they will never be too extreme in their emotional outlook. They will appreciate (and may even marry) people whose feelings are very different from their own, and defend their right to express those feelings, without necessarily agreeing with them.

The Heart Line that rises with multiple tributaries on the Mount of Jupiter and between the mounts (figure 17D) is indicative of tolerance. Its wearers will not display an over-fondness for money and material goods, though they will not be slow to accept any that come their way. They are rarely 'bad' people, but they will not be too strictly bound by laws or moral codes; they are usually keen to test new ideas, to 'try anything once'. Their personality will not seem as powerful as some; they are multi-faceted and the more interesting for that. They can be very loyal, even when the subject of their loyalty does not seem to deserve their devotion.

Not a few people have a three-tributary Heart Line, tapping

all three points and blending them equally. Once the basic principles, the qualities of Jupiter and Saturn, are understood, an interpretation can be made accordingly. But much will depend too on the nature of the Head Line, the habitual thought patterns, and the keenness of the subject's brain.

Signs on the Heart Line

A Heart Line that is firm and clear, without blemishes, suggests an emotional life that runs similarly along a smooth course. Partners and associates will always know where they stand with the wearer of an unmarked and unremarkable Heart Line. In palmistry, distinctive signs along the Heart Line are the outward and visible symbols of characteristics which interrupt the smooth and unremarkable flow of emotions and, in disrupting it, frequently cause problems for friends and loved ones, who may be driven to look for motives that are not really there. If you have an inbuilt tendency to 'fly off the handle' now and then, you will not need a real reason; you will always be able to find one to fit the case.

Signs along the Heart Line, then, do not represent solid, material reasons for experiencing emotional problems; they represent an inbuilt propensity for allowing difficulties to arise, a peculiarity in the individual flow of feelings. Many Heart Lines have the appearance of a chain rather than a clearly marked line, along some or all of their length (figure 18A). We began by picturing the Heart Line as a river flowing from the mounts. Now suppose that river to be littered with boulders. The water will swirl this way and that, splashing and eddying, as it finds its way across the plain. This is a symbolic picture of a person with a chained Heart Line; such a person may seem to be highly emotional, and their emotions will be wildly unpredictable. We all know people like that — we may even be a little like that ourselves! Friends and marriage partners have to learn to live with it, or look for a change of partner; they cannot alter the trait itself.

It is not simply the love life or family relationships of that person that are liable to suffer. Unpredictable emotional outbursts

THE HEART LINE

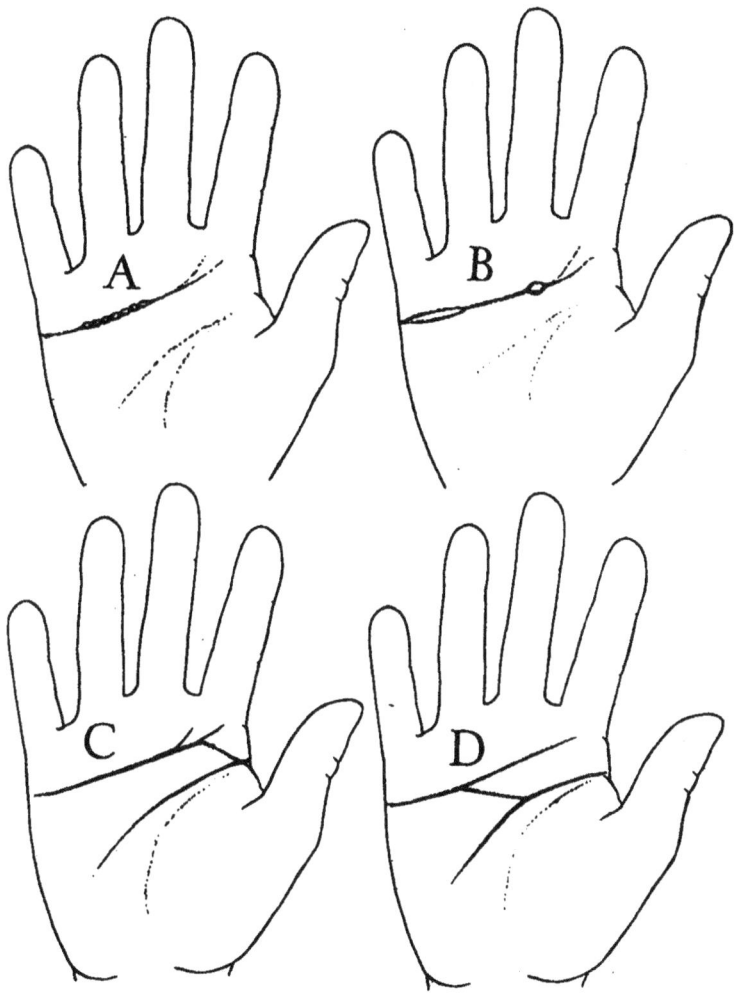

Figure 18
The Heart Line: (A) chained formation beneath the Mount of the Sun; (B) island below the Mount of Saturn and an elongated island below the Mount of Mercury; (C) an early link from Head to Heart Line; (D) link from Saturn Head Line to Sun Heart Line.

can affect business and social life as well, simply because no one can quite rely on any kind of arrangement that has an emotional base. If the Heart Line is only partly chained, take careful note of where, along the line, the chain formation occurs. Early chaining, beneath the Mount of Saturn, implies that the subject's sense of material values will be most affected. Possessions and money are themselves totally neutral, but they often seem to acquire an emotional fervour. Such a person will be erratic in his or her attitude to wealth and property, with a 'distorted sense of values'. They may be over-generous one minute, bafflingly mean the next. Seemingly worthless items may be amassed with magpie-like enthusiasm or, possibly, even valuable goods may be discarded without apparent thought.

A Heart Line chain beneath the Mount of the Sun implies that emotional unpredictability will be evident in the field of abstract possessions: of ideas, of prestige, of art and its appreciation. Such a person may decide that a piece of rubbish, or an old tin can, or a dead animal, has suddenly become an object of art to be admired and discussed — and if he or she happens to be influential enough, others round about may actually believe it! Then again, a Heart Line chain beneath the Mount of the Sun may indicate that its wearer tends to act in ways that attract notoriety rather than acclaim — he or she decides to become a villain rather than a hero or heroine.

A chained formation on the Heart Line where it passes beneath the Mount of Mercury implies that emotional instability will make itself known chiefly in the sphere of communication. Occasionally you meet someone for whom everything seems to run smoothly, and they will be at peace with the world, until someone asks them an innocent question, only to get a completely unexpected put-down as a reply. 'What did I say?' is a remark to be heard, not from the wearer of this sign, but from the people with whom he or she comes into contact. Or they may be eager to speak out in public debate, ony to miss the point entirely. Such a person is not being stupid or deliberately awkward. It is simply that, in their case, the emotional base of communication has become tangled and confused.

An island formation (figure 18B) on the Heart Line implies

THE HEART LINE

a degree of emotional isolation. It may be quite small and round, or elongated and extensive. The former is usually taken to indicate some isolated event that has made or is to make a profound impact on the subject's emotional life. It is the traditional sign of an unhappy romance. A long island, which makes the Heart Line appear double-tracked along much of its length, implies that this state of affairs has very deep and long-lasting effects. The effect of an island in a river is to divide the waters so that two streams run simultaneously, more or less parallel, and by inference this is what happens to the emotions when some obstacle gets in the way.

But of course there are an almost infinite number of circumstances and events that can happen to people, and only a very limited number and variety of signs on the hand to depict them. Your interpretation will depend upon your own train of thought, and your subject's expectations. In the case of your own hand, you will probably already be well aware of the nature of any emotional obstacles. All these and other signs along the Heart Line are summarised below.

Signs on the Heart Line

Star	Happiness; romance; good fortune.
Cross	Traumatic experience; misfortune.
Square	Able to absorb and overcome emotional hurts.
Triangle	Able to think your way out of emotional problems.
Island	Guilt; emotional stress. Refer to the nearest mount.
Parallel doubling	A secret side to your emotional life. Refer to the nearest mount.
Chained formation	Emotional instability. Refer to the nearest mount.
Breaks	Quarrelsome nature; emotional upsets.
Overlapping breaks	Tendency to fall out with partners only to make up later.
Crossbars	Emotional disturbances; interference in romantic life.

Links with the Head Line

The Head Line is discussed in the next chapter. In the case of most people, the two functions of thinking and feeling are clearly differentiated and actually do seem to run along widely separated tracks. In some others, however, the distinction is less clear. The two streams become combined at some point. Don't forget that we are visualising the three main lines of the hand as streams of vital awareness, flowing outwards from the area of the Mount of Jupiter. Rivers that begin as separate entities may flow together or, by forking, become divided on the plain. When the Heart Line forks, the lowermost prong running into the Head Line, this implies that part of what is normally an emotional function is habitually ruled by the power of logic, or rational calculation. This type of link will be covered in the next chapter. When a fork stems from the Head Line, however, the uppermost prong running into the Heart Line, the implication is that part of the logical function of the brain has become diverted so as to be subject to an emotional solution. It is this type of link that concerns us now.

Always note the point at which the fork or link leaves the one line and arrives at the other, in relation to the mounts above it. An early link rising from the Head Line to meet the Heart Line near its commencement around the Mount of Jupiter (figure 18C), is usually interpreted in terms of partnership. It implies that the subject's sense of ambition will be devoted largely to making a partnership work effectively, whether it involves marriage, or business, or both. Such single-minded devotion will allow nothing and no one to stand in the way, and it is a wonderful asset and reassuring omen if it appears in the hand of a prospective partner-for-life.

Money matters are normally dealt with by the brain, or logical thought, but a link from the Head Line which joins the Heart Line beneath the Mount of Saturn implies that, in this case, such matters will be delegated to the heart, or emotional feeling. This sign is often seen in the hands of people who consider material matters to be beneath their dignity. Their hearts may long

THE HEART LINE

wistfully for a lottery win, but their stern brains dismiss all such hopes as folly.

An early link which leaves the Head line beneath the Mount of Jupiter and joins the Heart Line beneath the Mount of the Sun is the mark of one who will stand no nonsense in the field of culture. Such a person will stick grimly to hard reality, and seldom indulge in day-dreaming about fame and fortune. This is no risk-taker; 'better the devil you know...' as far as he or she is concerned. Such a person will have no objection to anyone else holding their head in the clouds, however, and if they have children they will quite like the idea of them taking up all the illogical pursuits that they have denied themselves.

Now consider the effects of a link which leaves the Head Line where it passes beneath the Mount of Saturn and reaches the Heart Line beneath the Mount of the Sun (figure 18D). This time it is not the basic driving force of ambition that is being diverted into the emotional sphere: it is that part of the brain which should be dealing with material security, money and property, that is being delegated to the heart. Such people may well be ambitious, but when it comes down to the hard realities of life, soft abstract feelings keep taking over. They may manufacture beautiful products, and not bother to sell them; they may produce intellectual works of creative value, only to discard them. Others will say that these people lack a business brain, and they may make a good living out of exploiting them. Lacking the urge to grasp the solid, material value of their work, they are most unlikely to become rich themselves.

A link leaving the Head Line beneath the Mount of Saturn, joining the Heart Line beneath the Mount of Mercury, implies that material resources, matters with which the brain should be dealing, are being communicated and dispensed on emotional grounds. Compassion and generosity wll be shown in cases where common sense would call for discretion. Eventually, the subject's home and family may come to seem less important than the welfare of downtrodden strangers in some faraway land. This person should be reminded that charity begins at home.

Finally, there is the type of link which leaves the Head

THE ART OF PALMISTRY

Line more or less below the Mount of the Sun, and joins the Heart Line, again beneath the Mount of Mercury. This implies that matters concerning 'personal integration' or, more specifically, any problems that involve partnership and marriage, and which might in some cases be dealt with by common sense or the power of logic, are being transferred and communicated almost entirely by way of the emotions. The intellectual who falls in love with a totally unsuitable partner is likely to wear this sign. The heart will overrule the brain when any decisions are to be made regarding romantic liaisons.

'So you want a job with us — with *that* Head Line?
You must be joking!'

5
THE HEAD LINE

The flow of thoughts

The Head Line represents the workings of the brain, and by its clarity and orientation it can give us some idea of the kind of intelligence possessed by the owner of the hand. Length of the Head Line is a very rough guide to the standard of intellect. The cleverest people are said to have the longest Head Lines; but please don't be too dogmatic about this — consider it a general trend. If your own hand shows a very short Head Line, don't go through the rest of your life believing yourself to be an academic failure. Even if it is literally true, intellectual brilliance and common sense are two very different qualities, and short Head Liners may possess plenty of common sense.

    Depth and clarity of this line reflect the habitual clarity of thought, but not necessarily its 'depth'. A faint and shallow Head Line may belong to a woolly-minded person, but he or she may yet have very deep thoughts, whilst a clear-thinker, though well able to concentrate efficiently, may not care to ponder too deeply, and may seem superficial by comparison. The comparative clarity of the Head Line, however, will certainly offer a clue as to which function is the most important for the individual concerned.

    The direction of the Head Line carries more significance than either its length or depth. Remember the qualities ascribed to the mounts on the subjective (percussive) side of the palm, considering them from an intellectual rather than an emotional viewpoint. The Mount of the Sun expresses culture and integrity; the Mount of Mercury expresses communication and business sense; the Upper Mount of Mars expresses tenacity and practical determination; the Mount of the Moon expresses creativity, imagination, and intuition. All these factors can prove attractive to the mind. The Head Line, having started beneath the Mount of Jupiter, normally heads more or less straight across the palm at first, as though supported by the magnetic pull, the material force of the Mount of Saturn (from which, of course, the mind can never really escape). As it passes beneath this mount and enters the influence of the Mount of the Sun it reaches, as it were, a point of personal decision: in which direction, says the mind, does my true destiny lie?

Basically there are three clear choices: the Mount of Mercury is the seat of communication — in the emotional sense of fondness and compassion; in the intellectual sense of business acumen. Also, in positive vein, of medical practice; in negative vein, the manipulation and exploitation of others. The Head Line that is drawn upwards in this direction represents the kind of mind that tends to dwell on these things. The unusual configuration which results (figure 19A) has been called the 'Sign of the Moneymaker'.

The Upper Mount of Mars stands directly opposite the Head Line at its commencement, and if the characteristics which this mount represents prove a magnetic attraction, the line will appear markedly straight, sometimes reaching clean across the palm (figure 19B). Such a line is the mark of a logical, coolly calculating brain able to cling doggedly to the subject in question. Facts are paramount to this type of person, who tends to be quite intolerant of those who adhere less rigidly to logic. Other factors permitting, it is a good line to possess if your work calls for a determinedly unequivocal stance, and where facts and figures are all-important.

Finally, the Mount of the Moon may prove a magnetic attraction, for this, of course, is the seat of everything that is *not* hard and fast, not cut and dried, not bound by logical rules. The slightly woolly-minded majority of us probably feel more at home in the upper regions of this mount than elsewhere. We are then not too far removed from the qualities of logic and dogged concentration when these are required, but reasonably familiar too

THE HEAD LINE

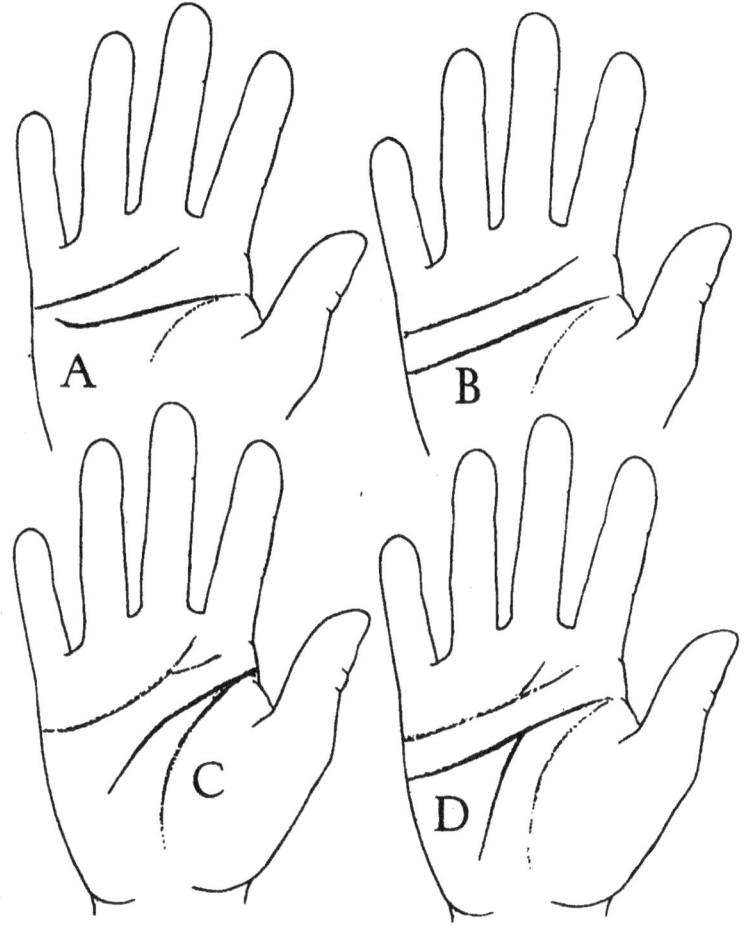

Figure 19
The Head Line: (A) straight Head Line curving upwards below the Mount of Mercury; (B) Straight Head Line running to the Upper Mount of Mars; (C) Head Line curving down to the Mount of the Moon; (D) a major fork on the Head Line.

with the more imaginative, artistic, sensitive side of life (see figure 19C).

A Head Line that plunges too deeply into the Mount of the Moon portrays a brain that seems to have cut itself off from the coldly factual side of life. Creative artists, mediums, seers, and all intuitive, sensitive people feel quite at home in these deep realms, but they are likely to be at a loss when faced with the reality of making a living, and the possibility of putting these creative qualities to practical use. A fork at the end of this type of Head Line could be a saving grace; it may signify a person who can make the best of both worlds. Small, multiple forks, by inference, indicate an ability to diversify, to taste and experience a correspondingly wide range of possibilities.

Some Head Lines divide half-way along, forking at the 'decision point' beneath the Mount of the Sun. The topmost prong of this major fork may explore the factual realms of the Upper Mount of Mars, even probing upwards towards the businesslike Mount of Mercury; the other prong may penetrate deeply into the Mount of the Moon, perhaps forking again as though to make best use of intuition and creativity. This is the mark of the all-rounder: basically, a person who can create, and sell the results; an inventor who can develop an invention and bring it to practical use. A major fork of this kind is illustrated in figure 19D.

The physical basis of thought

As with the Heart Line, all these factors may be modified by the rising point of the Head Line. In the majority of cases, the Head Line will be seen to rise slightly above the Life Line, so that it is lightly tied to it at its commencement (figure 20A). The brain with its capacity for thought does tend to be influenced quite considerably by the physical body, represented by the Life Line, by way of comfort, safety and personal living conditions. The heart by contrast, as represented by the Life Line, is scarcely attached to the body, and soars more readily to heights of its own. In effect, the emotions may wish to follow some course of action, but the logical

THE HEAD LINE

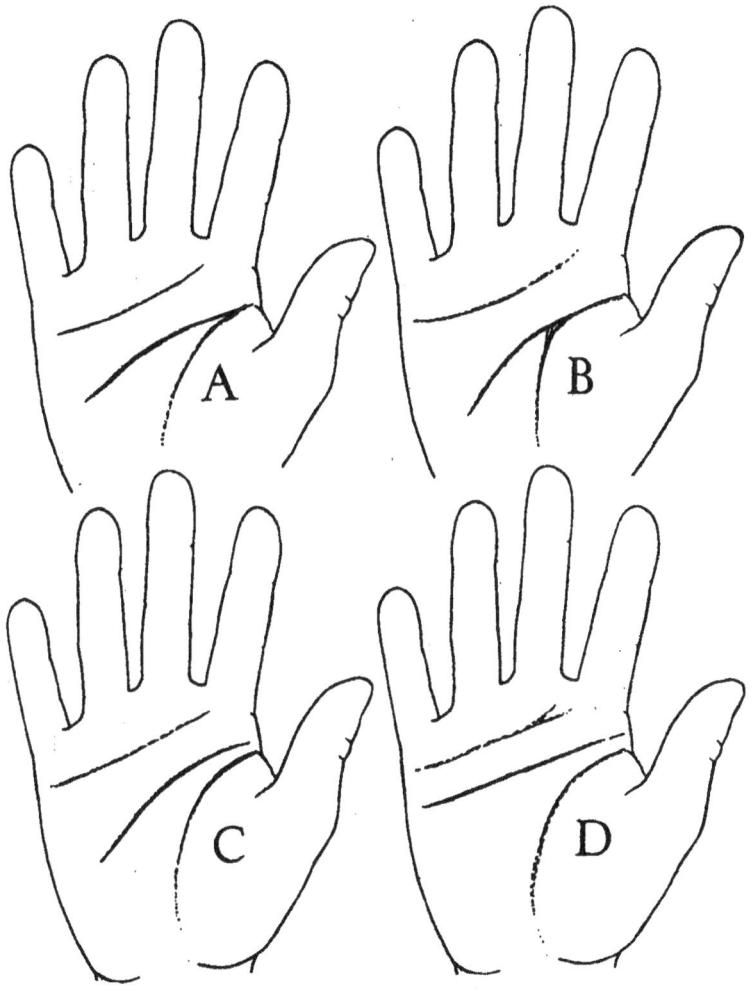

Figure 20
The Head Line: (A) lightly tied to the Life Line at its commencement; (B) heavily tied to the Life Line at its commencement; (C) widely separated from the Life Line, and downwards curving; (D) widely separated from the Life Line, and running straight across the palm.

part of the brain will say: Hang on; we may get hurt, or get into trouble, or get lost, or make a fool of ourselves. Let's wait a bit!

This is the normal, average state of affairs, and it is illustrated by the Head Line that is lightly tied to the Life Line for some length. In cases where this tie is pronounced, and continues for an inch, two centimetres or more, across the palm (figure 20B), it implies that this normal safeguard is exaggerated by the brain to the point of excessive caution — not merely in times of danger, but in ordinary social situations. Inhibitions will be evident in the wearer of such a protracted tie, often to the point of painful shyness: an extreme condition of psychological wariness.

A comparatively wide gap between the Head Line and the Life Line (figures 20C, D) will indicate the opposite extreme. With only a few minor tielines symbolically holding the brain to the body, this indicator belongs to the type of person who readily flings caution to the wind. It is natural for such a person to show physical bravery — not necessarily to become involved in bullets-flying situations, but able to make instant decisions, and willing to take part in activities which involve an element of risk, without pondering too deeply beforehand. Many physically-orientated games require at least a modicum of this quality.

The quality of bravery will be modified, of course, by its practical direction, indicated by the direction of the Head Line. When a Head Line, widely separated from the Life Line, heads straight across the palm towards the Upper Mount of Mars (see figure 20D), you can be fairly sure that this person lacks sentiment, or emotional affection. Don Quixote, the brave but foolish knight, typified this unusual human trait. The real person with such a trait may be friendly enough, but they will seem oddly detached. Separated from physical reality, their business ability will suffer, and worldly success will probably elude them.

It is a better omen when the Head Line which displays a widely separated start slopes gently down the palm to reach the Mount of the Moon (figure 20C). Such a person will be a deal more 'human', because their brains are not trying to take over the function of the heart, which will remain free to make its own value judgements. This type of bravery will always be held in check by a

THE HEAD LINE

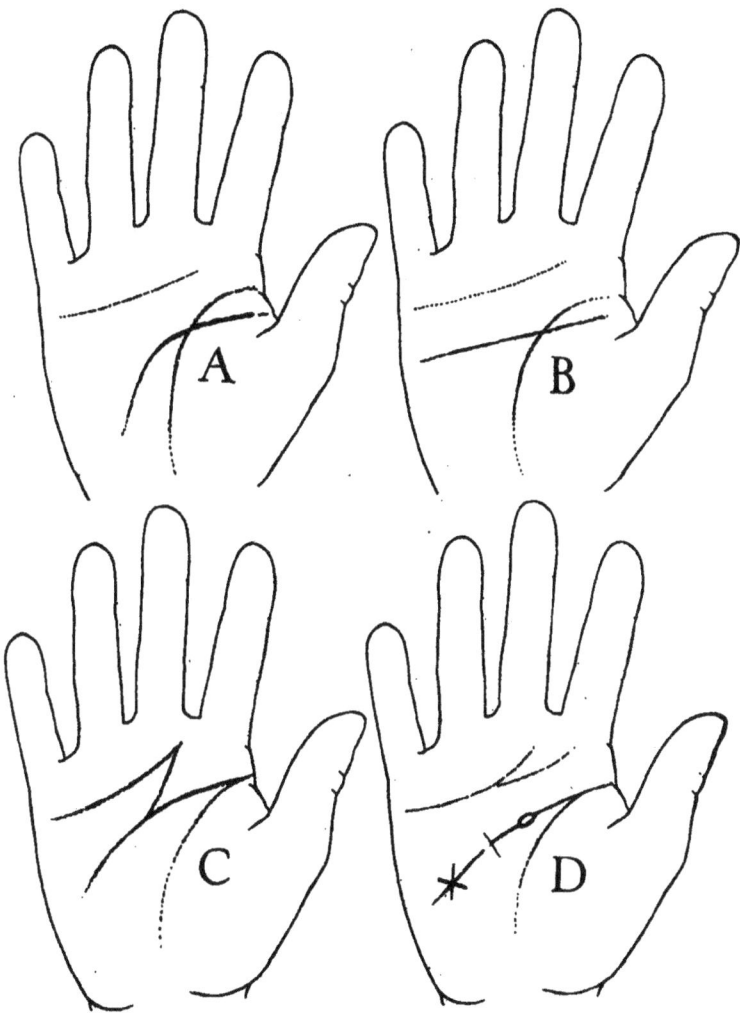

Figure 21
The Head Line: (A) rising within the Life Line, then plunging steeply; (B) rising within the Life Line, then running straight; (C) link from Heart Line to Saturn Head Line; (D) an island, a crossbar, a break and a cross on the Head Line.

constructive imagination, so that behaviour does not become too impulsive, too rash, too extreme, too 'Martian'.

So, by and large, bravery can be expected when the mind is powerfully motivated — that is, when the Head Line is that much closer to the Mount of Jupiter, and when it is not too closely concerned about physical welfare — and that is, when it is separated from the Life Line. But there is another direction in which the Head Line at its commencement may be separated from the Life Line: that is, when it rises on the Lower Mount of Mars, the seat of aggression, actually within the curve of the Life Line itself. This formation implies that physical aggression will rule the mind to the exclusion of rational restraint. In other words, it belongs to a thoroughly bad-tempered person. This is particularly true when the Head Line, having passed through the Life Line, dips quite steeply down to the Mount of the Moon (figure 21A); this is the warning sign of a 'rebel without a cause', an angry person who will not listen to reason. Should this Martian Head Line cross the palm more or less in a straight line, however, heading towards the abstract Upper Mount of Mars (figure 21B), this will balance out the Martian impulse. We can be reassured that this inbuilt anger, mitigated by common sense, will very likely be put to good use in the world of big business.

Tielines and signs

In the previous chapter we took note of tielines which rise from the Head Line to join the Heart Line, as though carrying some of the calculating workings of the brain into the more abstract field of emotion. Now we should consider tielines which run in the opposite direction, forking downwards from the Heart Line to meet the Head Line, as though channelling matters which would normally be dealt with by the heart so that they become non-emotional issues, subject to logical treatment by the mind.

Significant ties of this nature involving the Mount of Jupiter invariably imply that, as far as that particular subject is concerned, the head rules the heart; the sign of the logician. A

THE HEAD LINE

tieline leaving the Heart Line beneath the Mount of Saturn and striking the Head Line beneath the Mount of the Sun implies that the emotional valuation of things, sentimental values and suchlike feelings about material objects, have become carefully calculated matters of great importance to the person concerned, and tied up with the acquisition of wealth and property. Such a person may accumulate a vast store of goods, perhaps items which most others would regard with something like affectionate interest, old books and prints perhaps, pictures and various 'collectables'. With such a person, things like these are liable to become very important indeed.This could be the mark of a business person who specialises in the sale of *objets d'art*, valuing them for their potential profit rather than their beauty or curiosity.

Such Heart Line to Head Line ties can have powerful implications with regard to marriage too. Whereas an upwards tie beneath the Mount of Jupiter, carrying constructive thoughts to augment the emotions, can indicate a deep and lasting partnership based on devotion, a downwards tie at the same point suggests that marriage is not so much an emotional affair, but rather a matter of logical calculation. An early tie joining Heart Line to Head Line beneath the Mount of Saturn (figure 21C), inevitably suggests a marriage of convenience: not necessarily a cynical affair, nor necessarily a marriage for money, but certainly one in which the business and financial side of things will be left to the partner to deal with.

Island and chain formations along the Head Line may both be taken as possible indications of some kind of mental problem: the island an isolated illness, the chain a recurrent or long drawn-out disturbance. As with the Heart Line, we need to take note of the mount beneath which the sign appears, and take this as a clue to the seat of the problem, the area of the psyche where disturbed thoughts tend to congregate.

Obsessions of one sort or another often reveal their presence physically as an island in the Head Line. Beneath the Mount of Jupiter, the problem will lie within the field of ambition, of personal pride and the pursuit of power. Beneath the materially orientated Mount of Saturn, the disturbance will often be concerned with material acquisitions, wealth and property; but in cases where these things are not a problem, the formation is likely to indicate periods of depression and loss of confidence (figure 21D). Beneath the Mount of the Sun, an island can indicate problems in the sphere of social, cultural and spiritual attainment; depression may again be a feature, but there are more likely to be bouts of odd or antisocial behaviour. Beneath the Mount of Mercury (and of course this can apply only to a particularly long and comparatively straight Head Line), an island can sometimes indicate stress or even mental breakdown, brought on by studying too hard, or worrying too much about work.

The more thorough the interpretation, the better. Whilst a condition may prove serious and long-lasting, once the problem has been isolated, understood, and grasped, as it were, in the palm of the hand, it need no longer be a burden to the sufferer. The matter can more easily be put into perspective in the subject's life.

Some of the ensuing chapters cover the use of timescales, using in particular the Life Line and the Line of Fate. Both the Heart Line and the Head Line are taken to represent the heart and mind of the subject as a whole, an inherited inbuilt quality, and it is neither customary nor practical to allocate timescales directly to them. Nevertheless, it is sometimes possible to place a date on likely periods of mental or emotional disturbance. The hand should be examined carefully for any minor links or ties between one of these signs and another major line which does carry a timescale, for this may enable an age, or a year, to be linked to the problem.

When a timescale is being used in this way, it will often be found that a bar or minor linkline crosses the Head Line, or Heart Line, close to an island, a length of chain, or other warning sign, usually on the index finger side. This is known as the 'actual barrier', and is the point to be ascribed a date, if possible. If given a purely physical meaning, a barrier such as this may indicate an injury to the head or, strangely enough, to a leg or arm. At all events, it will relate to some sort of trauma, a mental shock. A star or break in the Head Line has a similar meaning (see figure 23), and it will be made clearer once the use of timescales has been developed.

THE HEAD LINE

In the absence of anything that may tie a warning sign to a timescale, tradition has it that the half of the Heart and Head Lines on the side of the index finger refers to the subject's younger years, up to the age of 35; the little finger side covers the second half of a person's life, from 35 onwards. This 'rule of thumb' will offer a very rough guide to the timing of events on these lines. Other signs which may be seen on the Head Line are summarised below.

Signs on the Head Line

Star	Injury by accident, usually to the head itself. A star at the end of the Head Line is traditionally associated with danger involving water.
Cross	Suspicious thoughts. Mental confusion.
Square	Resilience. Resistance to the long-term effects of stress.
Triangle	Great strength of mind. Refer to the nearest mount.
Island	Stress. Indecision. Migraine. Refer to the nearest mount.
Parallel doubling	Inconsistency. Unusual behaviour.
Chained formation	Mental breakdown. Stressful periods. Nervous disability. Refer to nearest mount.
Breaks	Trauma. Injury to head or limbs. Headaches.
Overlapping breaks	Temporary inconsistencies. Forgetfulness.
Crossbars	Loss of memory. Migraine. 'Actual barrier'.

6
THE LIFE LINE

Physical energy

After the Heart and the Head Lines, this third fixed primary line symbolises the physical course of an individual life, charting personal well-being, strength, vigour and general health. If this line is of full length, reaching to the topmost bracelet of the Rascette, deeply delineated and without distinctive signs, it betokens a life that can be expected to run along a similarly clear course, long, strong, and vigorous, without too many traumatic experiences. But if the Life Line is short, or faint, or interrupted by some of the signs which palmists recognise, you can be fairly sure that the subject's life will be characterised by a delicate constitution, or problems of ill health.

The Heart and the Head Lines are both seen as fixed indicators of the subject's emotional and mental characteristics. The Life Line may also be seen in this way, but it may in addition be seen as an ongoing record of a person's life, which can be set to a timescale (figure 22). This enables the palmist to put an approximate date on any irregularities that it may be seen to reveal.

A special sign of vigour, often to be seen in the hands of athletes and others for whom extreme physical activity is part of their daily routine, is an Inner Life Line (figure 23A). As the name implies, this is a doubling of the Life Line, so that it takes on the appearance of a tramline curving around the Lower Mount of Mars and the Mount of Venus. This inner reinforcement of the Life Line may be complete, or it may continue only part of the way — in which case the point at which it ends can prove very significant when measured on the timescale. It can register the time when an

THE LIFE LINE

energetic keep-fit expert decides to take up gentle country walks instead of exhausting aerobics; the point at which a touch of arthritis persuades the weightlifter to sell his weights and start to take more interest in the garden.

Avoid being too dogmatic about anything you read in the hand; remember that palmistry is an art, and not a science. The Life Line may, for example, end short of its normal goal at the Rascette, but this must not be taken to indicate that its wearer's life is due to end at that point on the timescale. One thing we cannot do is to predict a time of death, and we should never even consider trying to do so. There are so many factors involved in a person's life, that mere physical vigour is not the be-all and end-all, Psychological and spiritual factors, both known and unknown, are all very much involved in the mysterious process of living. Determination can keep one person going long after another apparently more healthy individual has finally thrown in the towel.

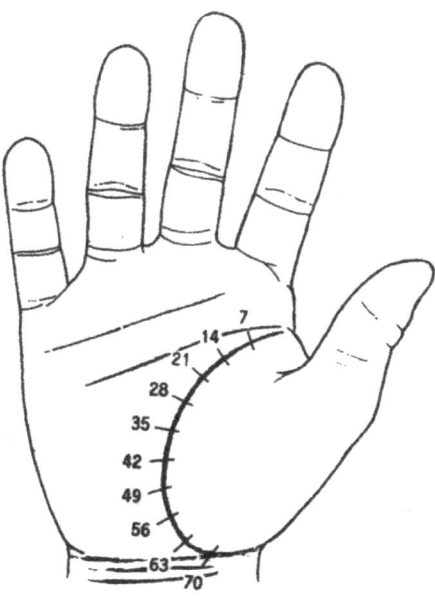

Figure 22

The Life Line: timescale.

THE ART OF PALMISTRY

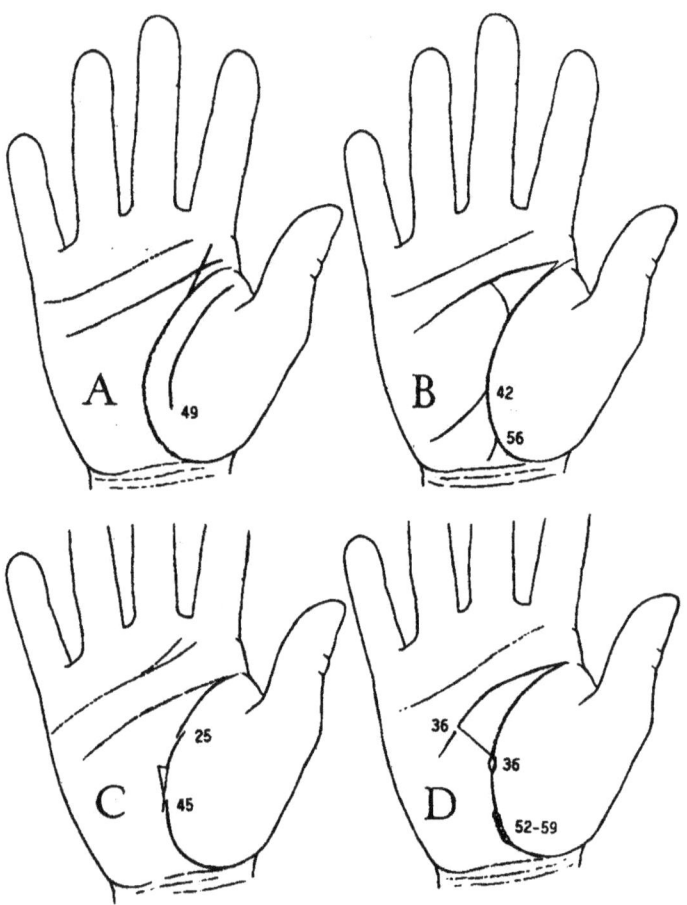

Figure 23
The Life Line: (A) initially tied to the Mount of Jupiter, with Inner Life Line running out at the age of 49; (B) backwards tie of inheritance, undated, and forks indicating disruptions to lifestyle at the ages of 42 and 56; (C) overlapping breaks at the ages of 25 and 45, and a triangle on the line; (D) island in the Life Line with a tieline to a break in the Head Line, marking an illness at the age of 36, with a chained formation between the ages of 52 and 59.

THE LIFE LINE

Another name for the Inner Life Line is the Line of Mars, and it certainly could be said to rise on the Lower Mount of Mars, the seat of vigour and physical aggression. It represents a particular brand of physical stubbornness, a refusal to give in. People who have attained a great age but are still active and vigorous are fairly certain to possess a Line of Mars, as the symbol of an inner strength that protects them against the debilitating effects of any problems fate might bring.

The Mount of Jupiter is the symbolic source of determination in all departments of life, but it is not a very good omen when the Life Line commences actually upon this mount. This high rising point suggests that the emotional and mental well-being of that individual is likely to be in some way impaired, that their psychic energy is being channelled instead into a physical outlet. However, a tributary or minor tieline linking the Life Line at its commencement with the Mount of Jupiter (figure 23A) is a good portent of dynamism, pride and ambition being expressed in a physical way. Athletes who value physical competition will wear such a link as a badge of success.

Timescales

There are various methods of plotting a timescale, and palmists tend to have their own favourite. My system is based on the seven-year stages of development. Most people experience a distinct change in their own being, their psychological centre of gravity, their awareness of health, which takes place every seven years. In some it is very noticeable; in others it is far less pronounced, but it is common to all. It is easier to appreciate these changes if you are of fairly advanced years yourself, because you can readily look back on your own life and recall the periodic changes in your own way of thinking, your own varying interests and social attitudes. The precise nature of these changes will be different for us all. The following is a general account of possible experiences.

As a very young child, up to the age of 7, your functions are governed chiefly by instinct: your brain and emotions are not yet properly developed; your experience of life is purely subjective and completely dependent on others as your selfhood develops. Then as you pass the seven-year milestone, and until you reach the age of 14, your chief psychological function, the 'compartment of consciousness' developing faster and being used more frequently than other factors, is emotional feeling. Instinct no longer works for you, and you have no use for it. Your views on life are still largely subjective, but your ego is growing daily.

By tradition, puberty is said to arrive at 14 years of age, and at all events this is a very significant time in your life. You are developing physically and you view the world more objectively, though with some apprehension. You are still not sure of how you are to fit into the world, and you may suffer from feelings of insecurity. When your 21st birthday arrives you are due to go through another change. Your brain may be fully in charge of your own life, but you are not really independent; you still rely on parents, home and inherited values, whether you realise it or not, and you are likely to experience a sense of limitation.

Twenty-eight years of age is an important turning point in anyone's life. At last you feel you can drop all the old parental restraints and launch out on your own, doing all the things you did not feel free to do before. The faculty of intuition is now working in you and, as you build your own future, you may gain insights previously undreamed of. When you get to be 35, your character goes through another deep change. You again become an emotional rather than an intuitive person, and you are likely to acquire a completely new concept of yourself, of your real value in the world, of your true individuality. You find new interests and new activities.

As you reach 42, the emotional certainties which you have acquired over the past seven years seem to have evaporated again, and you will be actively seeking a new lifestyle, a new outlet for your energy. Although you have reached what many would call the middle years, you probably feel more physically orientated, more energetic, than you have at any time since your teenage years; as often as not, you will be able to put this newfound energy to profitable use. Many people at this time of life seek a change of

THE LIFE LINE

career, or have change thrust upon them, and as a rule this is all to the good.

Approaching the end of your forties, a strange thing is liable to happen: quite suddenly you lose your physical drive and become a much more thoughtful person. Where your bodily sensations have been calling the tune in recent years, your brain now calls a halt, and you will probably find yourself seeking a more cerebral outlet for your ambitions. Your social aims, too, are raised a notch as you become more aware of your potentialities. The chances are that you will not be able to satisfy these aims fully, however, and you may feel increasingly frustrated intellectually as this seven-year period draws to a close.

As you pass your 56th birthday, you may come to feel that you have reached an important milestone in your career. Your recent ambitions may have been thwarted because you were depending too much on your own brain-power, but now the old and half-forgotten power of intuition takes over. Yet again you switch direction to find a new outlet, a new ambition, frequently dumping projects which you have begun, following some course that had not occurred to you before, looking always to the future.

The next seven-year stage takes you to 63: time to stop briefly and take stock of what has been done so far. You need to give yourself a break from onerous duty, and indulge your deepest feelings, finding some sort of practical emotional outlet for your energy. Quite suddenly it may occur to you, too, that you are no longer young; that your days are numbered, but instead of apprehension this realisation creates a new sense of peace within. You find yourself thinking that it would be very desirable to do something really worthwhile with the time you have left, and your emotional efforts will be set with this in mind. You may well live past your century, of course, and as I have pointed out already, the hand cannot indicate the age of death. But, as far as palmistry is concerned, and as far as the timescales on the lines of your hand are able to register, your time runs out at 70. Further psychological changes cannot be traced in the hand. If you want to go more deeply into these matters you need to study the so-called 'Grand Cycle', which is explained in my book *The Handbook of Palmistry*.

Lines of Influence

The Mount of Venus represents home and family, as well as sensual relationships, so it can readily be appreciated that minor lines, or 'Lines of Influence' which arise within this area and reach or cross the Life Line, are said to transmit influences of this nature. We have already seen how both concentric and radiating lines within the curve of the Life Line can represent romantic liaisons. Lines of Influence which arise more or less at random on the Mount of Venus, and travel to or beyond the Life Line, usually represent the influence of family members.

A line of this sort which crosses the Life Line to reach and touch the Head Line symbolises the kind of family support that is freely available, especially during the subject's youthful years. The timescale at the point of crossing the Life Line can give some idea of when this kind of help is most needed and most likely to be provided. When a Line of Influence begins at the Life Line, sweeping upwards from it and curving to join the Head Line, a 'backwards link', it is most likely to refer to financial support such as an inheritance (figure 23B). Tradition insists that no timescale date can or should be set on a Line of Inheritance. An inheritance often involves somebody's death, and as we have already seen, a death is not something that may be predicted, either through palmistry or by any other reputable means.

Minor tielines joining the Life Line and the Head Line near their commencement also carry the significance of parental and family support, but only whilst the subject is still a teenager. They indicate that a happy family environment, having sustained the subject during childhood, will give way smoothly and gradually over a period of years to a state of psychological independence. Lines of this nature connecting the Life and the Head Lines are not such a good omen when they cross both the Head and the Heart Line (at its commencement) to reach the Mount of Saturn. The implication here is that any benefits which might have arisen through family influence will be lost; life for the subject concerned, during his or her early years of independence at least, is likely to prove a financial struggle.

THE LIFE LINE

A Line of Influence which crosses the Life Line and reaches as far as the Mount of the Sun will represent what may seem to the individual at the time to be of negative value, but it will in fact lead to the best possible long-term results. It suggests that inherited talents will be put to good use, resulting in success and public acclaim. Remember that these backwards links point to a circumstance and not a date; it is not possible to apply the timescale to their point of departure from the Life Line.

There may be many minor lines arising from, or finishing at, the Life Line, and as a rule they cannot all be ascribed a hard and fast meaning. But when you bear in mind the various psychological changes to which we are all heir at various fairly predictable and definite times in our lives, you will see that even minor lines can readily be interpreted according to both the subject's expectations, and the palmist's train of thought. This is not cheating, by the way; such points in the subject's life will truly refer to significant times, happenings and changes of perception. Together they can form an interesting and accurate sketch of an individual life.

This type of general interpretation, involving multiple possibilities, should be brought into play when the Life Line bears a fork or series of minor forks, where it rounds the base of the Mount of Venus. Irregularities such as these refer to the somewhat disruptive time in the lives of most people, as the timescale will show. Most likely periods for forks and disruptions are during the early forties, and a few years later as the fifties commence. Changes of psychological perception and physical direction will be charted by these configurations, and for an elderly person they will be changes that are still to the forefront of the memory. Anyone who has not yet reached middle age can be gently forewarned of the changes and disruptions that are to be expected, and may usually be reassured that a seemingly stormy passage will be safely weathered (see figure 23B).

Lines which run like minor forks from the Life Line towards the Mount of the Moon, usually in the left palm, are often termed 'Travel Lines'. Quite often, they may refer to periods of residence abroad. I would say, however, that their literal connection with travel will only be evident where an actual journey has had a very deep significance for the person concerned. Once upon a time, journeys abroad were unusual. Nowadays, however, most people travel widely, quickly and easily, covering journeys that would have seemed amazing a few generations ago. Experiences that would probably have had a deep psychological impact on travellers then, will scarcely register in the mind of a typical package tourist now. That, I suppose, is progress. But it means that 'Travel Lines' in the hand need to be interpreted with caution. They should be taken to symbolise journeys of the mind, or of the soul, rather than of the body alone: periods of psychological change; new insights and new understandings (see figure 23B).

Signs on the Life Line

Star	Trauma. Accident. Refer to the timescale.
Cross	Period of hardship. Refer to the timescale.
Square	Difficulties will be safely overcome. Particularly significant when surrounding a break or other sign.
Triangle	General indication of intelligence. Diplomatic lifestyle. Not usually subject to timing.
Island	Usually denotes a severe illness or period of depression. Refer to the timescale.
Parallel doubling	Not to be confused with an Inner Life Line. Period of confusion, quandary or insecurity. Refer to the timescale.
Chained formation	Period of severe stress or nervous disability. Sometimes denotes a recurrent illness. Refer to the timescale.
Breaks	Isolated illness. Refer to the timescale.
Overlapping breaks	Imply complete recovery from illness.
Crossbars	Periods of depression. Refer to the timescale.
Tielines	Connecting timescale with indications elsewhere.

THE LIFE LINE

Other signs on the Life Line

The clarity or otherwise of the Life Line is taken to reflect the general conditions of the subject. As with all major lines, it should be firmly and fairly deeply marked, and of a normal colour in relation to its wearer's general skin-tone. A Life Line that is noticeably pale or faint suggests a delicate constitution; patches of discoloration, too, can have a medical connotation. Clean breaks in what would otherwise be a healthy Life Line frequently indicate periods of physical illness. Illnesses of an emotional or psychological nature are more likely to be marked by an island, while a chained formation usually indicates some sort of protracted or frequently recurring nervous disability. Where the Life Line varies in depth, or shows a faintly marked stretch, the chances are that the subject has experienced, or is due to undergo, a particularly stressful period. All these indications can be given an approximate date by reference to the timescale. Other signs which may be seen on the Life Line are listed in the table opposite.

'Well, if you *must* know, your Life Line runs out — precisely — NOW!'

7
THE LINE OF FATE

Timing the events of fate

The first of the three lines of unconscious influence, the Line of Fate varies quite considerably from person to person. In some palms it may be clear and deep – well 'tied'. In many others it will be absent altogether. In the majority of cases it will be present, but only fairly faintly, and often with an erratic course. A complete Line of Fate typically commences at the topmost bracelet of the Rascette, and finishes on the Mount of Saturn — the seat of materiality; it symbolises the ups and downs of fate, all the unexpected happenings which have a solidly material effect on the individual, both physically and psychologically. It is particularly significant in the case of an individual who is independent, and responsible in the eyes of the world for his or her own actions.

Certain sorts of people are relatively unlikely to possess a clear Line of Fate: those who live their lives entirely under the influence of some organisation greater than themselves, and from which they can be said to draw their fate; or peasants, perhaps, who are completely dominated by the social or tribal rules under which they live; or even sophisticated people who happen to be dominated by their families for the whole of their lives; anyone who is not really free to do their own thing, whose will and fate are subjugated to the will of 'big brother'. To this list we can add those few people who, like saints or prophets, seem to have risen above earthly matters. All the rest of us do possess this line to a greater or lesser degree. When we do, we can set a timescale to it, enabling us to put an approximate date on the most important things that are fated to happen to us during our lives.

THE LINE OF FATE

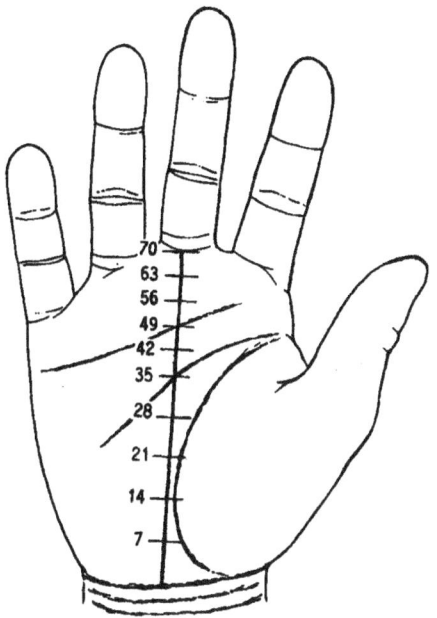

Figure 24

The Line of Fate: timescale.

The most successful people in life, in the practical, material sense, are the ones most likely to possess a clearly defined, comparatively straight Line of Fate. As a diagram symbolic of fate, this line should show at a glance whether a person's fate seems for them to be clearly mapped out. Some people seem able to stride confidently through life, apparently always knowing what to do for the best, and actually getting it done. Others seem to veer this way and that, going uncertainly through life, forever trying and usually failing to find a clear track ahead. We probably know instinctively to which category we ourselves belong; our friends and relatives are certain to know it, and the Line of Fate in our palms, by its clarity and directness, should bear it out.

The timescale should always be set so that the age of 35 corresponds with the crossing-point of the Head Line, and the age of 49 with that of the Heart Line. These two points between the extremities of birth at the topmost bracelet, and the age of 70 at the base of the second finger, form the cardinal points. The plan of the first half of a person's life, from birth to 35, will as a rule be widely spaced by comparison with the second half. As people age, it becomes increasingly difficult, or more challenging, to place the events of fate against the course of their life. Time in any case always seems to go faster when somebody is past middle age, and to move very slowly indeed for 'youngsters' under the age of 35!

The actual finishing point of the Line of Fate, typically the Mount of Saturn, also has significance: the point at which fate seems finally to have lost its power. But quite often the line varies from its standard course, veers at a certain point and heads for another goal. A Line of Fate that ends on the Mount of Jupiter (see figure 25D) implies that from the age indicated on the scale at the change of direction, material fate has somehow become diverted into the field of ambition. Such a person may never grow rich, but their worldly ambitions are fairly certain to be fulfilled. A Line of Fate that swerves the other way and ends on the Mount of the Sun implies that success through the hand of fate will apply within the sphere of culture and prestige. This is a sign likely to be found in the hand of a highly popular personality for whom public acclaim seems essential. Occasionally the Line of Fate will be found to veer even more widely and approach or reach the Mount of Mercury. In this case, fate will seem to have taken a hand in the fields of business and public relations, or, equally well, in science or medicine. Solidly material and especially financial success in the subject's professional life will seem to be effortlessly achieved.

Forks in the Line of Fate always tend to imply potentialities that are dissipated or diluted. All-rounders may well possess a Line of Fate that forks at some point along the timescale, and touches two or more mounts, indicating their broad range of interests, but the chances are that financial success will elude them. Minor, multiple forks on the Mount of Saturn itself also suggest scattering of the material benefits implied by a strong Line of Fate,

THE LINE OF FATE

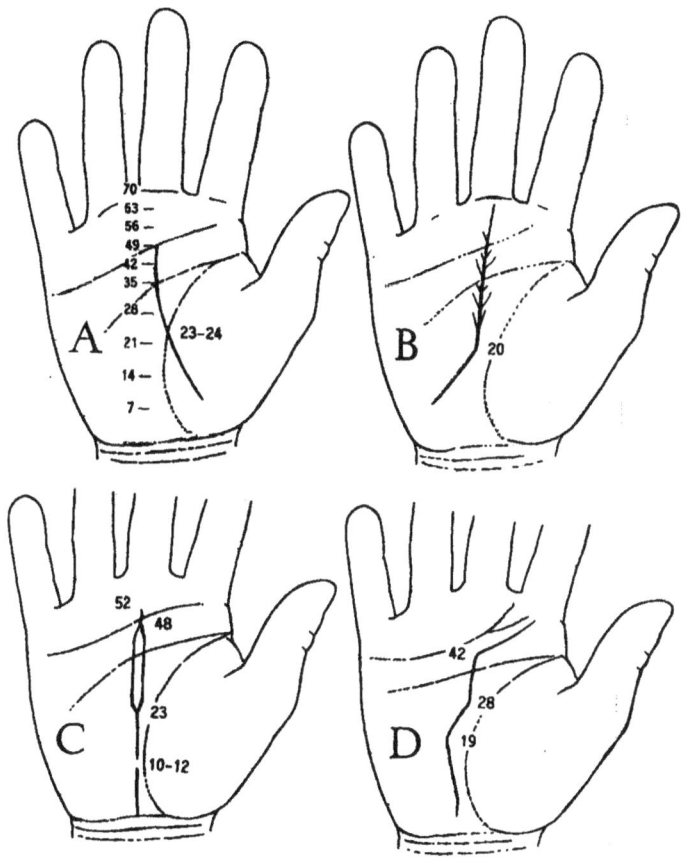

Figure 25

The Line of Fate: (A) showing how the timescale should run its full length, irrespective of the actual rising and finishing points, leaving the family circle at the age of 23-24; (B) rising on the Mount of the Moon, outside influence taking effect at the age of 20, with ascending herringbone lines; (C) break shows severe disruption at the age of 10-12, and an elongated island suggesting a 'double life' from the age of 23 to 48, fate running out at 52; (D) line ending on the Mount of Jupiter, with changes of direction at ages 19, 28 and 42.

particularly during the subject's later years, though they do suggest a wide and satisfying range of interests and skills. Conversely, when the Line of Fate runs singly, straight and clear to the base of the Saturn finger after having started late, perhaps on the Heart Line, the inference is a happy and comfortable old age.

Firm, clearly defined changes of direction, as distinct from an overall wavering Line of Fate, will often be found to correspond with important changes of occupation — and with them, changes of outlook — that take place during the subject's life. These can be dated fairly accurately on the timescale (see figure 25B). Never forget that the timescale should run its full course; that is, it should commence on the Rascette and end at the base of the Saturn finger, even though the line itself may not appear on the palm until much higher up, or (as in figure 25A) at a different point altogether; and the same applies when it finishes short, quite low on the palm.

Lines of Influence touching or approaching the Line of Fate always carry fateful implications, depending on their source, and they too may be, or seem to be, the cause of a major change of direction in the Line of Fate. Those most likely to be met with will be covered in the ensuing chapters. Numerous minor lines are sometimes evident, giving the Line of Fate a distinctive herringbone pattern, either rising or falling. Indeed, they may appear on the other lines of the hand too, and traditionally they are said to indicate the overall use to which resources and energy are habitually put. Descending lines suggest squandered resources, wasted energy. Ascending ones (figure 25B) indicate resources wisely spent and energy that is conserved and put to proper use. In general they suggest an overall attitude of mind for the person concerned: a 'positive' or a 'negative' one.

The typical rising point, signifying the point of birth, is the topmost bracelet of the Rascette. As we have already noted, this is the point at which the timescale should commence, although for many individuals the actual point at which the Line of Fate makes its appearance will differ. Its actual rising point along the timescale can be said to represent the time in a person's life when fate begins to take charge; the time when they leave a somewhat sheltered background, perhaps, and begin to make their way in a less readily forgiving world. Very often the Line of Fate will commence at

THE LINE OF FATE

some point along the Life Line. The area surrounded by the Life Line — the Mount of Venus — represents home and family background, and this point of departure marks the time, or age, at which the subject has at last become free from parental influences. Often, the Line of Fate may rise within the Life Line, actually on the Mount of Venus (figure 25A), and the interpretation here is that the home and family background has been a happy, secure and valuable one. But again, true independence does not begin until the Line of Fate breaks free from the surrounding Life Line. Many young adults are still 'tied to their mother's apron strings!'

Sometimes, the Line of Fate rises on the opposite side of the palm, on the Mount of the Moon. The Line of Fate, remember, carries only material implications of fate, so this cannot be interpreted as syphoning abstract, intuitional matters from the Mount of the Moon. The implication here is that non-family influences formed the most significant contribution to the subject's upbringing (see figure 25B).

Occasionally, the Line of Fate may be seen to commence in its usual place or close to the Rascette, only to merge with the Life Line for a time, or even to cross it and travel some way before re-emerging. The implication of this is that an otherwise normal childhood with early independence has encountered hampering circumstances which forced the subject to re-enter a state of dependence. Where the Line of Fate has actually penetrated the Life Line, it implies a change of structure or attitude within the subject's own family which has hampered independence. Where it merges and travels along the course of the Life Line for a while, it implies a family circumstance that is in some way a substitute for true parental care, with non-family people acting *in loco parentis*.

Divergence of Fate

Sometimes the Line of Fate is found to commence on the Mount of Venus, travel a short distance, and end as it touches the Life Line. This important line will seem to have been relegated to a mere Line of Influence. The unfortunate owner of such a line seems fated never to leave the sheltering background of parents and family, never really to attain the sort of independence that is essential for good relationships and a successful marriage. If marriage takes place, this configuration suggests the sort of union in which the parents or in-laws are always interfering, and the subject, rather than 'forsaking all others' as the marriage vows require, meekly allows these relatives to rule the roost.

Signs on the Line of Fate

Star	Risk of accident. Threats to material security. On timescale, referring to the indefinite ensuing period. Close to line: apparent setbacks with lucky consequences.
Cross	Trauma. Threat to career; loss of wealth. Low down and close to line, suggests family tragedy. Elsewhere on line, material gain (refer to timescale). High on the line on the Mount of Saturn: 'Mark of the Scaffold' warning against reckless behaviour. On line between Heart and Head Lines: the 'Mystic Cross'.
Square	Good arising out of hardship. Protection against threats to wellbeing.
Triangle	Intellectual prowess overcoming financial difficulties. At base of line: 'Mark of Mercy' or morbidity.
Parallel doubling	Implying a double life; a side of the personality being kept secret. Refer to timescale.
Island	Financial difficulties. Refer to timescale.
Chained formation	Unforseen difficulties; period of insecurity. Refer to timescale.
Breaks	Disruptions to lifestyle. Refer to timescale.
Overlapping breaks	Temporary upheavals in routine. Refer to timescale.
Crossbars	Drain on financial resources. Refer to timescale.
Changes of direction	Changes of occupation or lifestyle. Refer to timescale. Wavering course implies negativity, wasted energy.

THE LINE OF FATE

For a Line of Fate to commence late or finish early is not necessarily either 'good' or 'bad'. It depends largely on the sort of life the subject has led in the past and wants to lead in the future. As a rule, more things 'happen' to a person while their Line of Fate is present in their hand according to the timescale; corresponding, that is, with the current course of their life. The point at which a person finds his or her feet in the sense of success, the right job, the greatest contentment — this may well be the point at which the Line of Fate ends. In this case, once the happy connection has been made, they are their own masters or mistresses, and their fate will be largely self-made. For an overall 'successful' person, this can only be good. For a not-so-successful one, having been abandoned by fate can be rather bad. You will see that there can be no hard and fast rules; your interpretation must depend on the person involved. Even more so than with the other lines of the hand, minor signs can have far-reaching significance when they appear on the Line of Fate. They are summarised in the table opposite.

'Oh, don't worry. Look, I've got PRECISELY the same mark on my hand.'

8
THE LINE OF FORTUNE

Success and self-regard

The second of the three lines of unconscious influence, the Line of Fortune, is less frequently to be seen than the Line of Fate. Like the latter, it commences at the topmost bracelet of the Rascette, but runs to the Mount of the Sun; for this reason it is often called the Line of the Sun, or the Sun Line. Traditional palmists maintain that only eminently successful people possess this line clearly defined in its entirety. The majority of people, those who do not possess a clear Line of Fortune, they say, are unlikely to attain the full fruits of success, in terms of prestige and wealth.

Obviously, in one sense, this is true. No one, so far as I know, has contacted a statistical sample of lottery winners to enquire whether or not they possess this line, and I predict that if they were to do so the results would prove negative. Material wealth and its acquisition is more likely to be reflected along the Line of Fate, with its connotation of materiality. The type of success represented by the Line of Fortune has a more emotional nature than that expressed by the Line of Fate: an element of success for the feelings rather than for the body or the intellect. It is more concerned with abstract wealth: public acclaim and prestige, success in the eyes of others. An unconscious influence working towards emotional satisfaction; feeling good with oneself and with the world.

Stars of stage and television are most likely to possess a well-formed Line of Fortune; but so, for that matter, are the most notorious gangsters, for they certainly are looked upon with something approaching awe — not so far removed from respect —

THE LINE OF FORTUNE

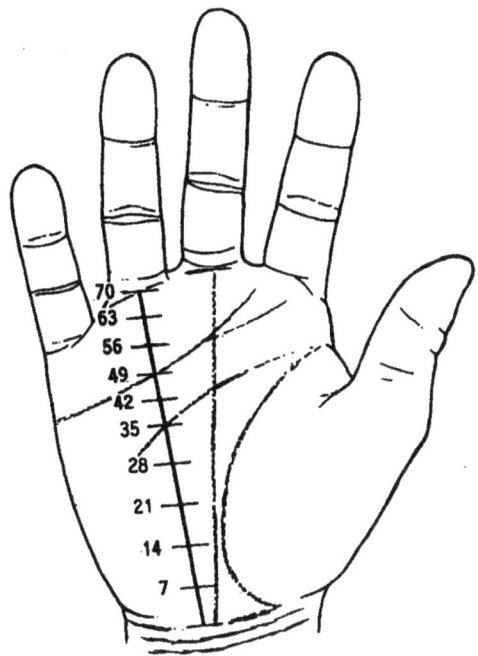

Figure 26

The Line of Fortune: timescale.

in the eyes of the people on whom they prey. They are likely, too, to feel well pleased with themselves. Sun Line people, in other words, are fated to succeed in whatever enterprise they have taken up, and succeed in such a way that others may envy, admire, or even fear them. These are the people most in tune with their own self-esteem, their own personal integration. Following ancient tradition, Asian palmists sometimes refer to it as the 'King Line', and claim that it is worn by those of royal blood. I cannot confirm this. However I do know that the most highly spiritual person I have known, a true prophet of the twentieth century, possessed a powerful Line of Fortune, rising on the Mount of the Moon at the age on the timescale at which he had received his revelation.

Like the Line of Fate, the Line of Fortune can be provided with a timescale, which runs from birth, at the Rascette, through the age of 35 where it meets the Head Line, 49 where it crosses the Heart Line, to 70 as it touches the base of the Sun finger. In the case of the majority of hands which display this line, it tends to appear, albeit faintly, at some point along its proper course, often emerging from the Line of Fate, and running only part of the way; but, as with the Line of Fate, the timescale should always be read as though the line were complete (figure 26).

The rising point of the Line of Fortune, when it varies from the norm, is particularly significant. Like the Line of Fate, it may sometimes rise within the Life Line on the Mount of Venus, implying that parents and family background will have done much to assist the establishment of success and prestige. A rising point on the opposite side of the palm, on the Mount of the Moon, signifies that outsiders rather than family members will have afforded the necessary boost towards fame and fortune; in this case, members of the opposite sex are particularly likely to have exerted useful influence, and established the right kind of confidence, at an early age.

The Line of Fate often provides a rising point for the Line of Fortune, so that it takes on the appearance of a fork rising from the Line of Fate itself (as in figure 27A), and the actual point at which it springs from this line should be noted carefully. If the timescale shows the event to have been in the subject's past, the date will usually prove to have a significance that will be well known to them: the beginning of true independence; a significant and fortuitous breakthrough within their chosen profession; the commencement of self-employment that turns out to be outstandingly worthwhile. From this rising point on, there will be no further dependence on anyone — and neither will there be anybody to blame if things go wrong. The subject will be captain of his or her own ship.

Conversely, fortune may seem to have run out abruptly when the Line of Fortune, despite having started strongly, suddenly fades away without forking. A fork may seem to record a similar occurrence: good fortune may appear to have flown as far as the subject's career is concerned. But this unconscious influence will

THE LINE OF FORTUNE

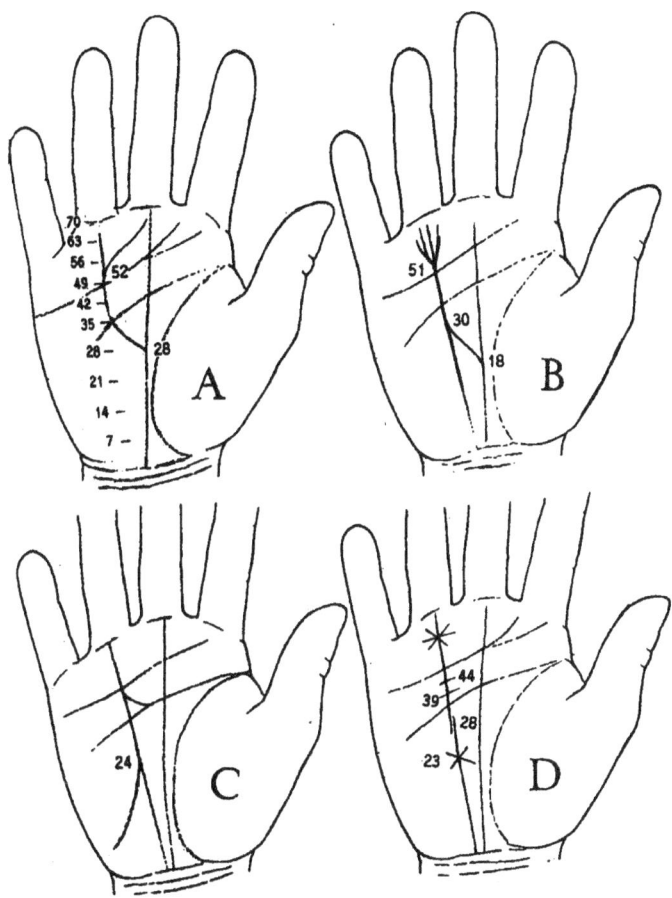

Figure 27

The Line of Fortune: (A) rising on the Line of Fate at the age of 28, forking towards the Mount of Saturn at the age of 52; (B) with a tieline from the Line of Fate, partnership commenced at the age of 18, with favourable results at the age of 30, multiple forking and diversification of career at age 51; (C) influence from a member of the opposite sex boosts career at age of 24, and a major successful business gamble is indicated by a link from the Head Line; (D) crosses and crossbars indicate threats to reputation at ages 23, 39, and 44, with a setback safely overcome at the age of 28; overall success predicted by a star on the Mount of the Sun.

simply have become more widely spread, bringing compensation in other fields of endeavour. Multiple forking (figure 27B) certainly may indicate that 'fortune' is being spread so widely that it may scarcely be evident at all. A major fork, however, particularly when the two prongs head for adjacent mounts, will have a positive connotation. Whereas the Mount of the Sun implies personal integration in the sense of emotional satisfaction and self-regard, a Line of Fortune that forks to touch the Mount of Mercury symbolises the transfer of some of that success into business and profitable public relations, or even the great gift of healing. A fork in the other direction, touching the Mount of Saturn, with its implication of materiality, suggests solid security, and success of the kind that will ensure substantial material rewards (figure 27A).

A Line of Fortune that rises very late — it may be on the Heart Line — and then travels to the base of the Sun finger, is an excellent omen of serenity and lack of want during the subject's later years; a golden retirement, surrounded by admirers and a loving family. But even a much-forked Line of Fortune, following a late start, implies an alert mind in a healthy body, both necessities for happiness in old age. For an unattached person, such a line forecasts a late marriage or partnership that will be happy and successful, particularly if there are corresponding indications in the hand by way of a Marriage Line (covered in chapter 10).

Another favourable pattern of partnership connected with the Line of Fortune makes its appearance as a tieline or branch running upwards from the Line of Fate to meet and join the Line of Fortune, and this may be given an approximate date by means of the timescale (see figure 27B). The omen is not at all favourable, however, when such a line cuts right through the Line of Fortune. The implication here is that the apparent partner merely wishes to share in the 'fortune', and may well turn out to be a confidence trickster of some sort — though of course other features may modify this.

People in whose hand the Line of Fortune is well developed are usually not averse to taking chances, particularly so when their Sun finger is long compared with its neighbours, and if they have a taste for gambling they are likely to be successful at it.

THE LINE OF FORTUNE

A prediction that is particularly relevant here may be made when a branch or minor fork from the Head Line joins the Line of Fortune. This line will represent just such a venture, a major gamble that 'seemed like a good idea at the time'. If such a tieline joins the Line of Fortune without actually cutting it, the outcome should be successful; but if it does bisect the line so as to form a cross, the venture is liable to end in disaster. It is a general warning, and no date should be set upon it by means of the Line of Fortune timescale. Other minor signs associated with the Line of Fortune are summarised below.

Signs on the Line of Fortune

Star	A sign of good fortune, particularly at the top of the line on the Mount of the Sun, where it is known as the 'Star of Success'.
Cross	Antagonism from envious people. Threat to reputation. Refer to timescale.
Square	Ability to overcome any threats to prestige.
Triangle	Ability to apply intellect to achieve success.
Parallel doubling	Implies a potentially scandalous situation being kept secret from the public. Refer to timescale.
Island	Sudden loss of prestige. Drain on resources. Refer to timescale.
Chained formation	Pursuing a scandalous course. Apparent seeking of notoriety. Refer to timescale.
Breaks	Failure of enterprise. Refer to timescale.
Overlapping breaks	Severe but temporary setbacks, successfully overcome. Refer to timescale.
Crossbars	Personal attacks threatening prestige.
Changes of direction	Changes in career. Refer to timescale.

9
THE LINE OF INTUITION

The third impersonal influence

We have seen that the Line of Fate symbolises a channel for those influences which affect material resources — the hard and fast happenings of fate, while the Line of Fortune represents those unconscious influences which affect matters of emotional well-being and prestige — one's cultural integrity. The Line of Intuition forms the symbolic channel for ideas, and more mysterious influences from the collective unconscious, when they are able to be received directly into the brain. From the Mount of Mercury these images can be communicated consciously as thoughts, hunches, or 'feelings', through the normal mental processes.

Jung categorised people into four classes, depending upon which basic function seemed to be used most often by them: there are *thinking* types, who chiefly make use of their thoughts; *feeling* types, who chiefly make use of their emotional function; *sensation* types, who chiefly make use of the physical 'impact' of things and ideas in their perception of the world; and lastly the *intuitional* types. Such people, in whom this impersonal influence is so well developed that they use it habitually in their normal everyday dealings, in whom it is more important even than the ordinary workings of their brain, their emotions and their body, are rare birds indeed.

It is probable, however, that most people use the function of intuition to a certain extent, from time to time. In particular, people at the forefront of public affairs — statesmen, ministers, generals, business managers —all need to use this strange gift, and they are usually well endowed with the capacity to do so. They do

THE LINE OF INTUITION

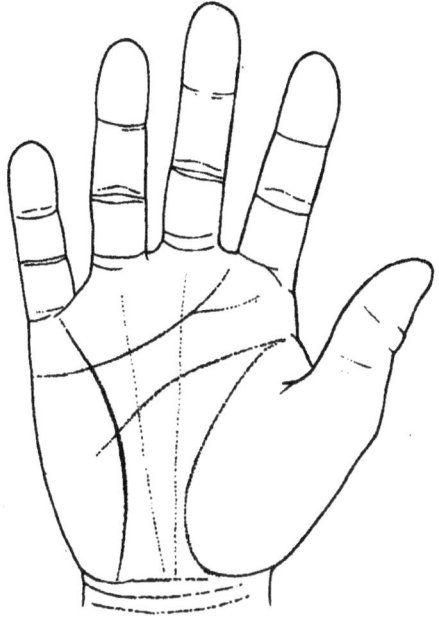

Figure 28

The line of Intuition: full length.

not think of themselves as 'psychic'. People who need to know what other people want, what their interests are, also make use of intuition: successful interviewers, writers and salespeople, as well as psychologists, doctors and nurses, they too need to develop this function as far as they can. Their capacity to do so will show in their hand, mapped out by the Line of Intuition.

A full-length Line of Intuition, one that reaches from the topmost bracelet of the Rascette all the way to the base of the little finger, is a rare sight. Indeed, we could say that it, or its wearer, equates to Jung's intuitional type. In some ways intuition is a primitive faculty, for it represents pure instinct without benefit of learning; but it can also be seen as a subtle development of the everyday functions of thinking and feeling. The fact is, in the vast majority of cases, when it is present at all, the Line of Intuition forms a curve as though to outline the Moon of the Moon, and falls short of full length both at its rising and its finish. You will remember the analogy of the three lines of impersonal influence resembling pipelines penetrating the dam of the Rascette, which holds back the full flood of contents from the collective unconscious. A typical Line of Intuition, you may discover, rather than tapping this great dam directly, merely picks up a small amount of seepage from it; most of its flow derives from the Mount of the Moon itself.

As you will recall, the Mount of the Moon is representative of all that is most subjective within the human psyche; the closer to the wrist, the more 'unconscious', and thereby the more mysterious, its implied nature. It is the home of abstract values, of creativity and receptivity, the land of myth and fable and fairy story. The lower down the palm, in symbolic terms, the more 'psychic'; the higher up the palm, the more practical, solid and material, will be the nature of the 'intuition' symbolised by this line.

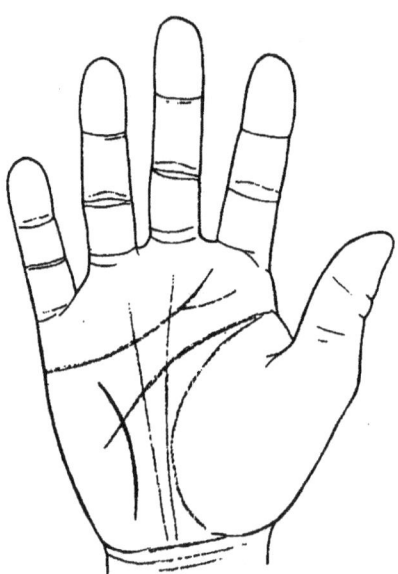

Figure 29
　　The Line of Intuition: short version denoting a vivid imagination.

THE LINE OF INTUITION

The Line of Intuition is a fixed line in that it cannot be given a timescale. Its starting point, as outlined above, is significant because it hints at the particular type of intuition being channelled. The finishing point is significant too, because it expresses the way in which intuition is being used. If the line stops short of the Upper Mount of Mars and peters out on the upper part of the Mount of the Moon, its possessor is unlikely to be able to put his or her imaginative ideas to practical use. This tends to be the badge of a head-in-the-clouds dreamer. However, when the Line of Intuition reaches the Upper Mount of Mars, the seat of tenacity and endurance, the products of a vivid imagination will prove to be of a tenacious and enduring value — they will be remembered and may be put to real use (figure 29).

When the Line of Intuition reaches as far as the Mount of Mercury it implies that all these abstract ideas can be communicated openly. Thus, a Line of Intuition which runs from low on the Mount of the Moon to the Mount of Mercury, particularly when it appears on the right hand, is the badge at least of a talented story-teller. But a Line of Intuition that runs its full course, from the topmost bracelet of the Rascette to the Mercury finger, suggests a strange character indeed: an intuitional type in whom the flow of weird images from the unconscious mind forms a natural part of consciousness; one in whom the unconventional and the eccentric will seem perfectly normal. Minor signs associated with this line are summarised below.

Signs on the Line of Intuition

Star	Extremely intuitive, a contented but impractical dreamer.
Cross	Antagonism brought about through misunderstandings.
Square	Profitable union between intuition and intellectual capacity.
Island	Unprofitable imagination; paranoia.
Chain	Brooding. Psychic imbalance.
Crossbars	Tendency to dwell on suspicions. Distrust.
Breaks	Absent-mindedness.

10
LOVE AND MARRIAGE

Affectionate relationships

The Marriage Line or lines are to be found near the edge of the palm, above the Heart Line. A timescale may be set to give an indication of the year involved. Assuming the Heart Line is fairly averagely disposed — and some Heart Lines, as we have seen, vary too greatly in length and direction to be of much use for this purpose — it should be taken as the base line. Using our seven-year scale, we have to follow the rule-of-thumb assumption that puberty occurs at 14 years of age, and that a person is subject to marriage, or a romantic liaison, from that age (see figure 30).

But Marriage Lines are not always very distinct, and even when they are particularly clearly defined, they are not completely reliable as forecasters or records of precise dates for marriage. However, they usually offer a fair guide to the most affectionate relationships, and particularly the long-term romantic relationships in a person's life. A single Marriage Line can usually be timed fairly confidently, but where there are several they do tend to be somewhat randomly distributed, except that in cases where there is a final, more lasting relationship or partnership following one or more previous relationships that did not last the course, it is always that final relationship that is likely to register accurately.

The Marriage Lines themselves make no distinction, of course, between a traditional white church wedding, a less formal registry office ceremony, or a simple statement of commitment, provided the relationship is really meaningful to the people concerned. Convention and public approval are not significant.

Bear in mind the part of the hand in which these lines

LOVE AND MARRIAGE

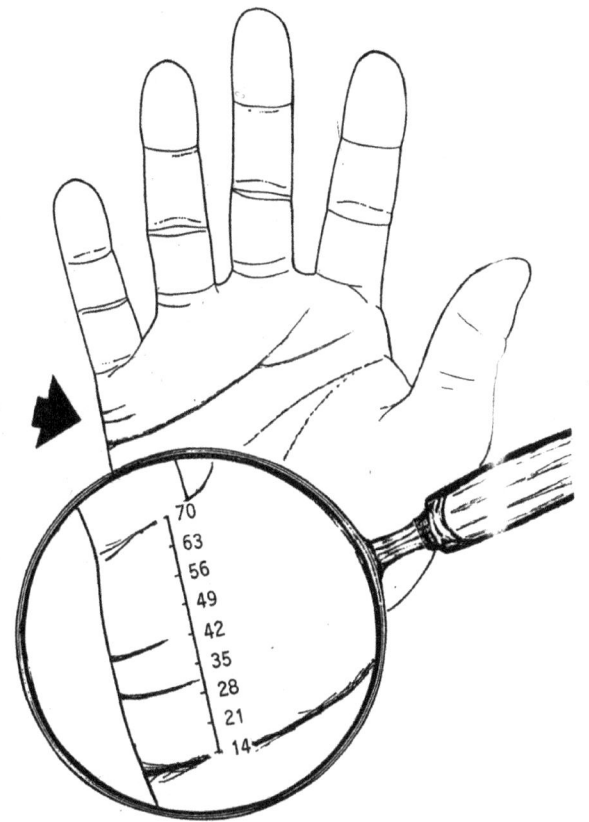

Figure 30
 The Marriage Lines: inset showing timescales.

occur, and the symbols which surround it: on the one side the culmination of the feelings is represented by the finishing point of the Heart Line, while on the other the qualities of communication and compassion are registered by the Mount of Mercury; both principles are operative here within the sphere of sexual maturity. This is the abstract side of the hand, the so-called percussion edge of the palm, and as such it cannot be expected to register precisely an event of material solidity. But it does register a consummation of the feelings, and the instinct to reproduce, a physical manifestation of these things happening simultaneously.

Child Lines are sometimes to be seen, usually limited to the uppermost Marriage Line if there are more than one. They consist of small, fine lines running down the Mount of Mercury to the base of the Marriage Line. It can be said that each represents a new sense of responsibility towards a personal creation, and they are very similar to the so-called Marks of Concern (see chapter 12). For this reason they may be seen on the hand of a childless person. Nevertheless they are usually significant within the context understood between the palmist and the subject. In the context of marriage, a boy is represented by a rather heavier or longer line than that for a girl, but they are not usually clear or accurate enough to differentiate between the offspring of separate marriages (see figure 34A).

Something about the nature of relationships as recorded by the Marriage Lines can be gleaned from a general study of the hand. A sensitive person who feels and notices details, or subtle shades of meaning in another's varying attitude towards them — such a person will own a hand that bears a complicated network of fine lines. They are people who need a partner with whom they are in intellectual as well as physical harmony.

The individual with a less complicated personality, one with straightforward feelings, one who will probably not notice or care about minor details and differences of opinion in their partner — this person's palm is likely to be unmarked apart from the basic lines, clearly etched. This latter type is the traditionalist, and as such is more likely to put up with a less than perfect relationship, because they feel they ought to follow the conventions of marriage and the rules of society. The former type, being more sensitive, is not at all interested in rules and conventions. They are more likely to anguish over their relationships, and if their Head Line suggests they are bold, imaginative thinkers, are far more likely to change partners, or to seek divorce; individual compatability is that much more important to them.

LOVE AND MARRIAGE

The Girdle of Venus

An Inner Heart Line, by inference, suggests a more subtle, inner type of feeling, and just such a line is often to be seen in the palms of sensitive people. It is usually known as the Girdle of Venus. In effect, the Marriage Lines themselves are representative of this Girdle on the edge of the palm, as though the expression of these most inward feelings comes to the surface and is recorded during that person's most intimate relationships. In the case of an individual in whose hand the Girdle of Venus is clearly marked, he or she is aware of these inner feelings most of the time. They seem to be transmitting deep feelings of affection in such a way that they are not directed at any one person, and are not necessarily of a sexual nature; there is always this awareness, this aura of attraction. Such people are often charming and fascinating, able to 'charm the birds off the trees'. They are idealists, nevertheless,

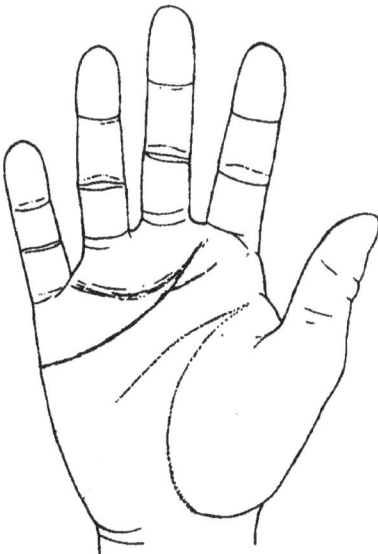

Figure 31

The Girdle of Venus: closed version.

always looking for the ideal partner. Physical relationships alone do not satisfy them, their emotions and their hopes run deep, and they tend to be subject to grave disappointments when their relationships turn out to be less than ideal.

There are two basic types of Girdle, the open, and the closed versions. The closed version (figure 31) surrounds the Mounts of Saturn and the Sun, ending between the sun and the Mercury fingers. The open version (figure 32) ends at the Marriage Line position, and looks rather like a series of disjointed Marriage Lines extending below the upper mounts, as an Inner Heart Line. This open version of the Girdle of Venus encloses the Mount of Mercury as though to embrace the communicative aspect of these inner feelings. People with the closed version, then, are likely to play their cards very close to their chests, and seldom let their true feelings slip. For this reason, some say that the sexual feelings of such people are repressed; but the truth is, their sexual proclivities and all their innermost feelings are very private, and for this reason are less likely to find outward expression.

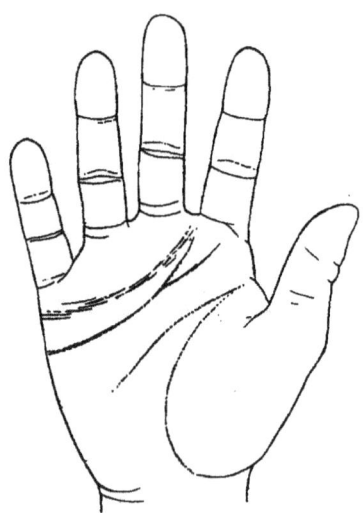

Figure 32

The Girdle of Venus: open version.

LOVE AND MARRIAGE

Difficult births

The Lower Girdle of Venus (figure 33) occurs at the least conscious part of the hand, and is an extension of the uppermost bracelet of the Rascette. Where the Upper Girdle of Venus expresses deep feelings as far as they are outgoing and being communicated to others, the Lower Girdle of Venus expresses the origin and embodiment of those feelings, their entry into the individual human psyche. This girdle represents something of a block or barrier to the assimilation of 'passions' in the broadest sense. On the symbolic level, it can imply that its wearer is slow to give birth or reality to new abstract ideas. When presented with some completely new concept, these people are liable to draw back and hesitate for longer than most. Waiting, it might seem, to see which way the cat is going to jump before committing themselves, they can be said to be on the defensive most of the time.

In a woman's hand, and in a far more practical sense, the Lower Girdle of Venus can sometimes indicate possible problems

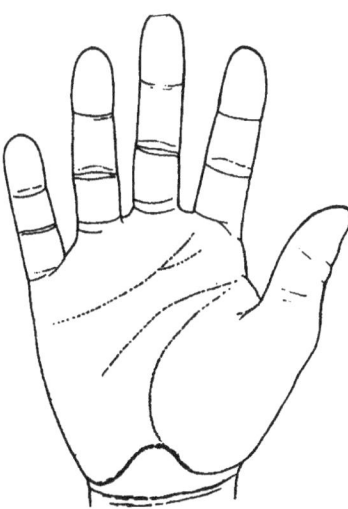

Figure 33
The Lower Girdle of Venus: an upwards loop of the topmost bracelet.

with childbirth, past, present or future. When it appears on the male hand it usually refers to its wearer's own birth. Caesarean babies are likely to bear this distinctive mark throughout their lives. It implies an unwillingness to be born — as though that symbolic dam wall is trying to hold back a newly emerging conscious being, not allowing it to leave the sea of the collective unconscious.

The quality of marriage

We have already seen in chapter 2 that various signs on the Mount of Venus have significance as indicators of the quality of a person's marriage. The Rising and Setting versions of the Star of Venus, for example (figure 34B), point to the difference between a romantic, passionate affair in which the chief concern is love and more love, and a more subdued, homely arrangement in which getting the children off to school, doing the housework, and looking after the old folks are the priorities. A star on the Heart Line points to happiness and serenity in marriage, in general terms, as does a star on the Marriage Line itself (see figure 34B).

  A cross on the Mount of Jupiter (figure 34B) can also be interpreted in a positive way. Crosses elsewhere on the hand usually depict opposition, with difficulties brought about through outside interference — particularly so when such a cross occurs on the Marriage Line itself (figure 34C). It implies that somebody may be working negatively behind the scenes to harm the relationship — probably not with actual malicious intent (for most people work towards the best as they see it), but in this case certainly with the likelihood of unpleasant consequences. But a cross on the Mount of Jupiter is very much a favourable sign, implying a good match in the sense that its wearer will not have to 'go it alone'; it entails a certain suppression or sacrifice of egoistic interests, but he or she will always be carried along in fine style by the strength of the partnership. The positive nature of this feature is greatly strengthened if there is also a star on the Mount of the Sun (see figure 34B).

  We also saw in chapter 2 that a sketchy history of minor romantic liaisons and their importance in a person's life may be

LOVE AND MARRIAGE

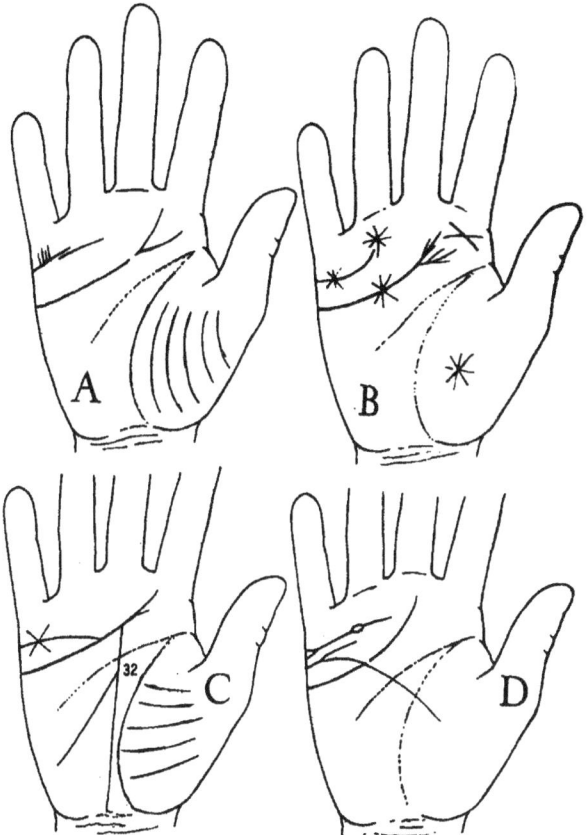

Figure 34

Marriage and romance: (A) the Marriage Line bears four Child Lines, respectively a girl, a boy, a girl, and another boy. The overlapping break indicates a temporary separation, the Heart Line break beneath the Mount of Saturn indicates emotional problems involving money, and the Mount of Venus bears signs of several romantic liaisons; (B) the Marriage Line is rising and starred, the Mount of Jupiter bears a cross, all signs of a happy marriage; (C) the Marriage Line bears a cross and slopes down to the Heart Line indicating a divorce, a Line of Influence from the Mount of the Moon indicates the arrival of a new partner at the age of 32, and the Mount of Venus bears the signs of several ongoing romantic interests; (D) two Marriage Lines, the earlier one forked, breaking the Heart Line and running to the Mount of Venus, suggesting emotional scenes and eventual divorce, the later one with tributaries indicating a strengthening relationship, and an island indicating deception.

read into the Lines of Influence often to be seen on the Mount of Venus. Those which curve to follow the course of the Life Line (figure 34A) each represent a former love who lives on in the wearer's heart, and evokes fond memories. Those lines which radiate from the base of the thumb (figure 34C) each represent a former partner (or a partner yet to be encountered) of a less romantic but also less fleeting, more practical nature. Their influence may still be felt negatively during the course of an otherwise happy marriage. A well-lined Mount of Venus is always the sign of a lusty person to whom romantic adventures are, or have been, the spice of life — provided they are not currently attached, of course!

The Marriage Lines usually vary between a person's left and right hands. The left hand shows the propensity for marriage that a person is born with; the right hand tends to show the actuality of it. The deeper significance of the left hand to right hand relationship is described in chapter 15. Ideally, a Marriage Line should be straight and fairly short (figure 35A, D). An over-long line hints at an over-emotional relationship, and it may be that the serious things of life, like making a living and acting responsibly, are not taken seriously enough. A Marriage Line that curves upward into the Mount of the Sun (figure 34B) betokens a long and happy relationship. A downwards curve is not such a good omen; if it runs into the Heart Line (as in figure 34C) it symbolises the likelihood of separation and divorce. At all events, and for whatever reason, it implies that the wearer of this down-curving line is likely to outlast or outlive his or her partner. Divorce is particularly likely to be the outcome if an over-long Marriage Line curves down and across the palm, reaching all the way to the Mount of Venus (figure 34D), for this link-up implies an inability to detach oneself from the old family ties. Such a marriage seems very unlikely to endure.

Where there is more than one Marriage Line, and it has been established that these refer to separate liaisons, the arrival of a second partner to replace the first may often be seen symbolised in the palm as a Line of Influence reaching the Line of Fate from the Mount of the Moon, expressing the powerful influence exerted by

LOVE AND MARRIAGE

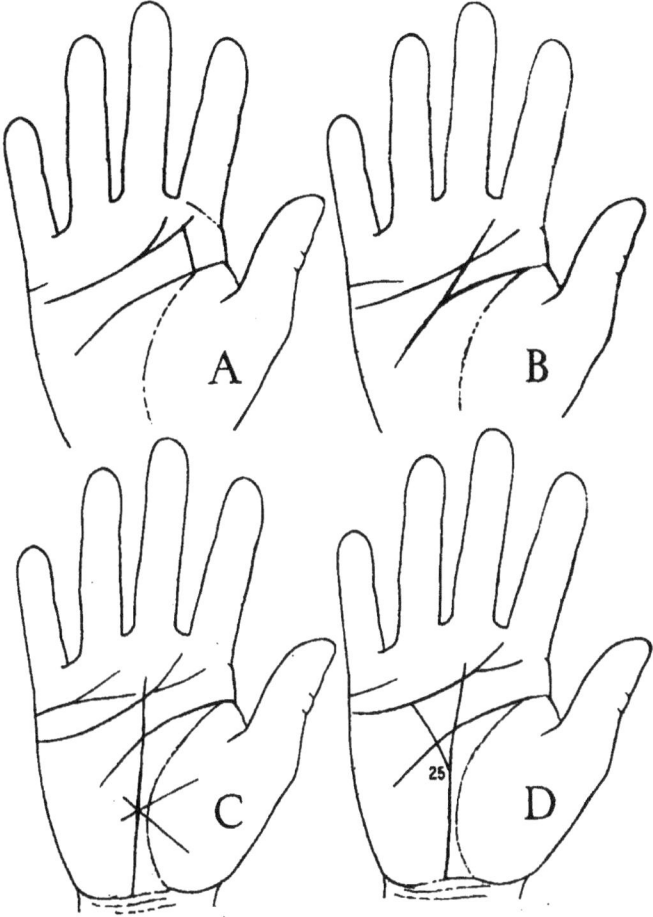

Figure 35
Marriage forecasts: (A) a rising link between Head and Heart Lines beneath the Mount of Jupiter indicates a lifelong, dedicated partnership; (B) a Heart to Head Line link beneath the Mount of Saturn, suggesting a one-sided and intolerant relationship; (C) a forked Marriage Line indicates a broad-minded relationship, or one with outside interests, and twin Lines of Influence from the Mount of Venus meeting in a cross on the Line of Fate suggest an 'eternal triangle'; (D) romance at the age of 25 leads to a successful marriage.

a particular person of the opposite sex, and the year or age of this happening may be read on the Line of Fate timescale (figure 34C).

A Marriage Line that starts with two tributaries on the percussion edge of the palm (figure 34D) implies that there are likely to be periods of involuntary separation and uncertainty for the first few years, but the relationship will develop and grow stronger as time passes. A break in the Marriage Line indicates an unforseen end to the partnership, though if the two broken ends overlap (figure 34A), the partners should be able to pick up the pieces again later, and start afresh. An island in the Marriage Line (figure 34D) is always taken to imply that some sort of deception is being practised by its wearer. His or her affections are running wildly in a circle, and they will probably feel guilty about it. An island usually warns of consequences more serious than a mere doubling of the line, which may mean no more than fond but harmless memories.

A Marriage Line that forks is not usually a bad sign. Frequently it implies that the two parties will get on well, without trying to dictate to each other. There will be a certain amount of freedom on both sides. An over-large fork in the Marriage Line, however (figure 34D), should always be taken as a warning for those concerned to refrain from the temptation of entering into some outside romantic attachment that is likely to harm the relationship. But for one who is already well into a secure second partnership, such a fork may simply mean that he or she still thinks very fondly of the first love — the partner that was lost.

As we have seen in chapter 4, the Heart Line can imply several things regarding marriage. One whose Heart Line rises on the Mount of Saturn (figure 34D) tends to have too strong a sense of ownership for the marriage to work well. They may prove unwilling to give themselves wholeheartedly to the partnership. A break in the Heart Line where it passes beneath the Mount of Saturn (figure 34A) implies that money, or the lack of it, is liable to cause marital problems. A break in the Heart Line beneath the Mount of the Sun (figure 34D) shows that more personal factors, conflicting interests, and in particular, perhaps, a conflict of sexual interests, do not really lend themselves to a happy and lasting partnership.

LOVE AND MARRIAGE

When marriage is very much on the subject's mind, the Heart Line can be taken to represent the spouse, or the marriage itself; the Head Line may be taken to represent the individual on whose hand it appears. These lines will then record his or her basic attitude towards the partnership. It comprises a different use of the symbols of palmistry, but there is no reason why the signs on the hand should not symbolise more than one thing at once. A tie-line linking the Head Line to the Heart Line in this context will imply that the individual submits his or her capacity for decision-making to the marriage — that is, to the partner. This can be gratifying when the partner enjoys making the decisions, and somewhat exasperating when they do not.

A Head Line link which meets the Heart Line beneath the Mount of Saturn means that all decisions involving cash and material security tend to be left to the spouse. A link joining beneath the Mount of the Sun means that all matters of outside entertainment and public life are delegated in this way. A link joining beneath the Mount of Mercury hints that the responsibility for socialising, entertaining, and business matters too, will be placed firmly on the shoulders of the spouse. Should the link leave the Head Line early, however, and rise almost straight to meet the Heart Line beneath the Mount of Jupiter, it means that the individual will devote his or her whole life to the marriage, so that their entire energy will be put into making the partnership work. This sign is frequently to be seen in the hands of self-employed couples who run their business together as a husband and wife team (see figure 35A).

The opposite in all these matters is to be assumed when the link is reversed, with a tie-line dropping from Heart to Head Line (figure 35B). For an unattached person, this type of link usually indicates that its wearer tends to overrule his or her emotions and place more reliance on cold logic when major decisions are to be confronted. But in the context of marriage, it is seen as implying that the subject tends to take from the partnership in a dictatorial manner rather than give. Gentleness, tolerance and understanding may seem to be lacking when the emotions are ignored in this way, and such a relationship, though it may function efficiently enough, will appear to be lacking in mutual love and respect.

Signs that may appear on the Marriage Lines are summarised below, but Lines of Influence often feature strongly when assessing the quality of a subject's marriage. Those that run from the Mount of Venus to touch the Line of Fate are taken to suggest interference from that person's family, usually from the parents. Whether the Line of Fate is actually present in the hand or not, when such a line continues up and across the palm to reach the Mount of Mercury, any chance of successful independence in marriage, without unwarranted interference from the parents, seems unlikely whilst they still live. Two Lines of Influence from the Mount of Venus, joining the Line of Fate at the same point, uniting so as to form a star or a cross, are usually taken to signify two contending lovers; an eternal triangle — or perhaps a vicious circle — but certainly an arrangement that is sure to end in tears (see figure 35C).

Signs on the Marriage Lines

Star	Serenity in marriage.
Cross	Opposition to marriage.
Square	Stable relationship overcoming threats from outside.
Triangle	Powerful intellect surmounting marital problems.
Island	Guilty secret. Extramarital affair.
Parallel doubling	Split loyalties, or fond and harmless memories.
Chain	Troubled over-emotional relationships.
Breaks	Separation.
Overlapping breaks	Separation followed by reconciliation.
Crossbars	Outside interference : threats to marital stability.
Tributaries	Initial period of separation, or dual loyalties.
Fork	Freedom from excessive ties, or split loyalties.
Downwards curve	Separation. Widowhood.
Upwards curve	Happy marriage.

LOVE AND MARRIAGE

Another method used by palmists to predict courtship and marriage is based on a branch-line rising from the Line of Fate and cutting through the Head Line (figure 35D). Its likely date can be estimated by the Line of Fate timescale. If such a line approaches but does not touch the Heart Line, though there will be a courtship, with a loving relationship, an actual wedding is unlikely to take place. If it touches the Heart Line without crossing it, it signifies a wedding that will prove happy; but if it cuts through the Heart Line, though the promised wedding will go ahead, it is unlikely to prove a very successful match.

'I realise you're not married, but I can still see in-law trouble on the way!'

11
HEALTH AND EXCESS

A line of ill health

In the case of ordinary, healthy people, the question of their own health seldom so much as comes to mind. This fact offers a clue as to the nature of the Line of Health, for fortunate people like these have no 'need' for this line, and seldom have one in fact. But when people are 'martyrs' to a condition, to a poor constitution, or if throughout their lives they suffer from recurrent health problems — or if in later years their general health begins to fail — from that time on they are sure to display a Line of Health clearly marked on their palm. So we can see that it measures ill health or sickness rather than health. It implies that the question of their personal health is normally present, occupying their awareness.

Since it carries this implication of thinking continually about health, the Line of Health can equally signify a predisposition towards hypochondria, as opposed to actual physical illness. Indeed, when the line is particularly direct and clear, this possibility may be considered a likelihood. It is the wavy, irregular, broken or otherwise signed Line of Health that is more likely to record physical illness. Only rarely is it a truly 'tied' line; if it is — well coloured and deeply defined — you can be sure that ill health has been a problem for its wearer since birth, and is probably a matter of inheritance. More usually, however, the Line of Health is absent from the hand during a person's youth, and only begins to make its appearance some time after middle age, slowly lengthening and deepening during the ensuing years as it travels up the palm.

HEALTH AND EXCESS

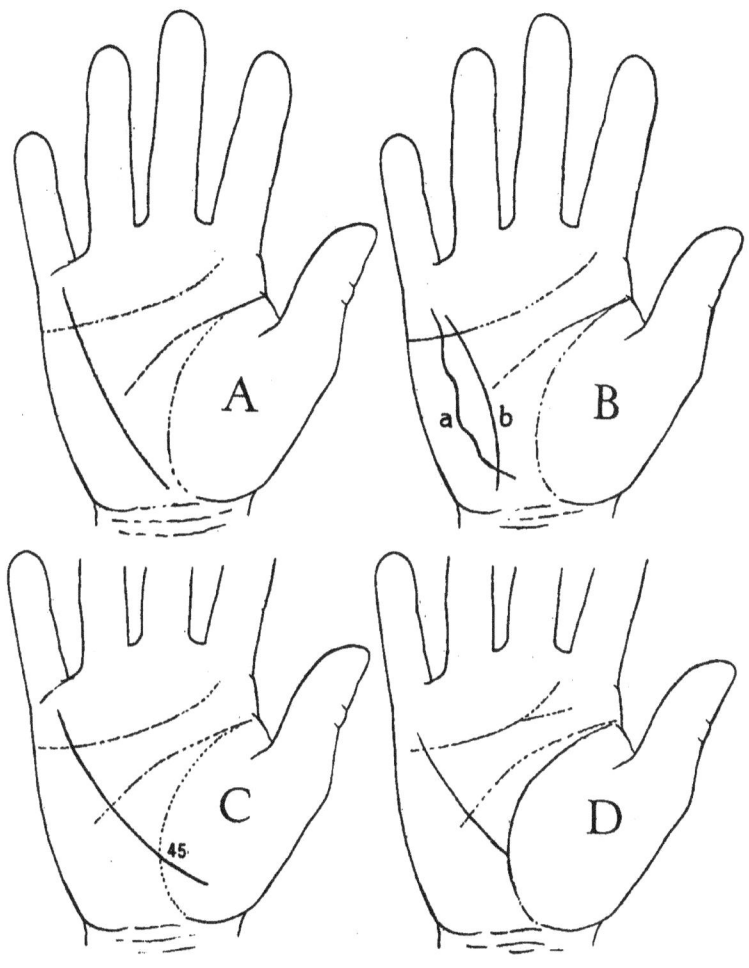

Figure 36
The Line of Health: (A) full-length version; (B) a) Line of Health, b) Line of Intuition; (C) rising on the Mount of Venus, indicating concern with health from the age of 45; (D) rising on the Life Line.

Some palmists say that the Line of Health rises at the top of the palm at the Mount of Mercury. Perhaps this is not important; but when it makes its appearance late in a person's life, it is usually the lower stretch, near the Rascette, that becomes evident first. The full normal course for this line runs from close to the Rascette, often from the Mount of Venus, occasionally from the Mount of the Moon, and from this point it usually curves as it crosses and climbs the palm, across the Moon of the Moon and the Upper Mount of Mars, to end up on the Mount of Mercury. The physical condition of its wearer can then truly be said to have permanently 'come to mind', so as to be constantly in their awareness. A full-length Line of Health is shown in figure 36A.

Should the Line of Health actually rise on the lower part of the Mount of the Moon, it may be confused with the Line of Intuition. But though the two lines in this case will seem to share both a rising point and a destination, the latter always curves in the outward direction, outlining the Mount of the Moon; the Line of Health tends to curve in the opposite, inward direction, towards the edge of the hand, often cutting across the Line of Intuition itself (figure 36B).

When the Line of Health rises on the Mount of Venus, as it frequently does, the point at which it cuts through the Life Line, with its timescale, can give some indication as to the age at which the subject's concern with matters of health is likely to set in; the age at which sensible measures to safeguard one's health ought to be taken (figure 36C).

A tied, genetically predisposed Line of Health is the more likely to bear distinctive signs that may indicate the type of ill health involved. The first characteristic to note relates to its firmness and continuity. A weak and wavering line usually points to problems with the digestive system — particularly so when it rises actually on the Life Line itself. This rising point is said to denote a habitual state of nervous tension, which usually brings about physical problems with the abdominal organs. The subject may be found to suffer from abdominal cramps, chronic indigestion and an acid stomach (figure 36D).

General debility is indicated by a much-broken Line of Health, like a series of dots and dashes (figure 37A). Islands in a

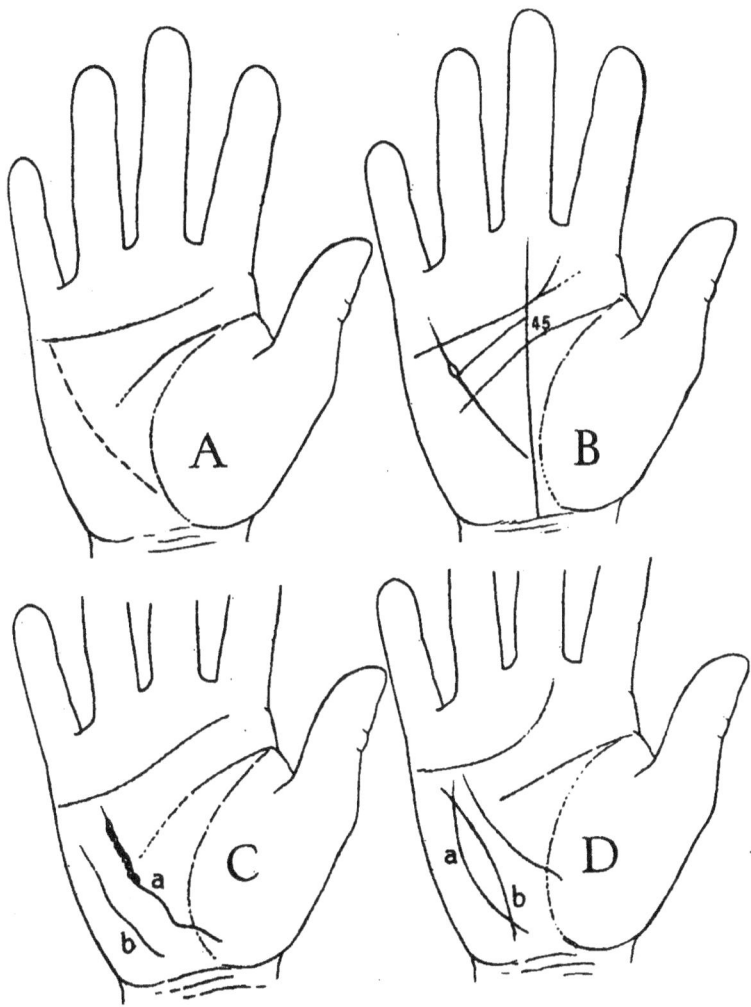

Figure 37
The Line of Health: (A) a broken Line of Health indicating general debility; (B) an island in the Line of Health indicating an internal condition, dated by a link with the Line of Fate at 45 years; (C) a) the Line of Health with a chained formation, b) the Line of Excess; (D) the Seal of Solomon below the Line of Health, a) Line of Excess, b) Line of Intuition.

firmly etched line are far more specific in their symbolism, and are usually taken to represent a potentially serious internal condition. A chained formation is usually said to denote a lung condition. There may be a timescale link with the Line of Fate that will indicate when these conditions are liable to cause trouble (see figure 37B).

In hands which show a clear Line of Health, there may be a lower or Inner Health Line, too (figure 37C). This is called the Line of Excess, and is said to indicate lascivious behaviour — it is sometimes known as the Lascivia — or sometimes a compulsive condition of medical deception: Munchausen's Syndrome. Perhaps it could be said to indicate emotional rather than physical ill health, for it certainly features most strongly when the subject is suspected of excessive indulgence, usually of an immoral, and always of a selfish nature. It could well denote a tendency towards addiction to confidence-enhancing drugs.

Sometimes the Line of Excess coincides exactly with the Line of Intuition, forming a pattern known as the Seal of Solomon (figure 37D). This unusual sign is sometimes found in the palm of an unscrupulous conman, the person who uses intuitionally acquired knowledge to bring about selfishly indulgent results, connected with sex, or money, or both: the ominous sign of a Svengali-like character of whom it would be as well to steer clear.

Signs on the Line of Health

Star	Sterility. Problems with childbirth.
Cross	Isolated serious illness.
Square	Serious health problems successfully overcome.
Triangle	Pondering over medical matters. Hypochondria.
Island	Serious internal illness.
Chain	Serious lung condition.
Breaks	General debility.
Overlapping breaks	Emotional rather than physical problems.
Crossbars	Recurrent illness.

12
SYMPATHY AND SENSITIVITY

Caring hands

The sensitive hand (figure 38) is certainly beautiful to look at, but its owner is not necessarily pliable and caring, so jump to no conclusions. It may be difficult imagining its owner doing heavy manual work or enjoying anything other than delicate, gentle pursuits, but things can rarely be so neatly pigeon-holed as that. An unscrupulous or even violent person may have delicate, slender hands. Caring, thoughtful, gentle people usually have fairly large, ungainly hands, with knobbly knuckles and blunt fingertips (figure 39). Perhaps basically there are two kinds of sensitivity: sensitivity to one's own needs and subtle perceptions, and sensitivity to the needs of others.

It would not be reasonable to conclude that the one attitude is selfish and the other unselfish, however, for both are reacting according to their own inbuilt needs, their own genetic programming. Ultimately, both are acting for themselves, on their own behalf, doing what they feel to be right — or at aleast unavoidable. Both types of hand may bear the same signs or marks of sensitivity, though your interpretation of each will need modification to suit the case.

The Line of Sympathy is a short but often deep line slanting across the Mount of Jupiter (figure 39C), It denotes the type of person who is apparently always ready to listen sympathetically to another's problems, and who will never try to 'top' someone else's difficulties with complaints of their own

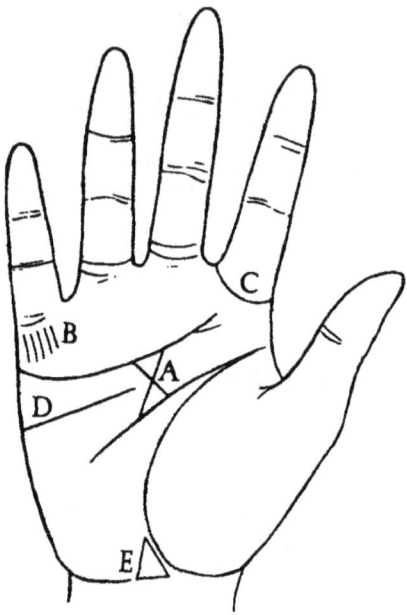

Figure 38
Sensitive, psychic hand: (A) the Mystic Cross; (B) the Marks of Concern; (C) the Ring of Solomon; (D) the Supernal Line; (E) the Mark of Morbidity (or Mercy).

(which, as we all know, can be an annoying habit). This characteristic is not entirely altruistic, however, for it denotes a somewhat private sort of person, one of those who keep their problems to themselves. They tend to be people who are good at keeping secrets, especially their own. Every good spy probably has a Line of Sympathy.

Very occasionally, as a modification of this sign, the so-called Ring of Solomon is to be seen surrounding the base of the Jupiter finger. Traditionally, the mythical ring of the biblical King Solomon himself is said to enable its wearer to talk with the animals. More significantly, its wearer is supposed to be able to transport himself or herself to celestial realms, to overcome supernatural opponents, even to gain the power to get a genie back into his bottle, which is a notoriously difficult thing to do. To

SYMPATHY AND SENSITIVITY

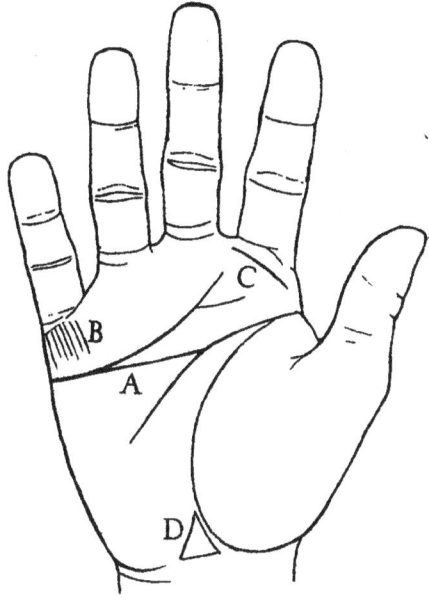

Figure 39
Practical, caring hand: (A) straight Head Line to Heart Line link; (B) Marks of Concern (Medical Stigmata); (C) Line of Sympathy; (D) Mark of Mercy (or Morbidity).

translate powers such as these into modern, understandable terms is almost equally difficult. But even if the symbol is only partially accurate, it is plain that we are talking about someone with unusual psychic gifts. If you happen to have such a sign yourself, or if you read the hands of someone else who has it, possibly you will understand or discover the true nature of these things (see figure 38C).

One sign which varies in its interpretation according to the cheirotype of its wearer is the Mark of Mercy, a clear and comparatively large triangle close to the base of the Life Line, between the Mounts of Venus and the Moon, just above the topmost bracelet of the Rascette. At best, and particularly when it occurs in the large hand of a caring person, this mark indicates compassion for the old, for the suffering and the dying, and the

127

unselfish willingness and ability to do something practical to help them. In the over-sensitive, willowy hand, where this mark is less commonly to be seen, it implies merely a morbid obsession with such matters, unpleasant thoughts of illness, incapacity and death. When this happens it is known, not as the Mark of Mercy, but as the Mark of Morbidity. It is illustrated in figures 38E and 39D.

The Marks of Concern are very similar to the Child Lines sometimes to be seen on the Marriage Line, but they are usually longer, and extend from the base of the little finger down the Mount of Mercury. The idea of all that it entails to have children should be borne in mind when interpeting this sign, for a child of one's own is, in a sense, one's own creation and one's own responsibility, as well as a unique object of love and concern. All this could equally well symbolise people who need care and attention, in the eyes of the wearer of this sign. It is often to be seen on the hands of doctors and nurses, and indeed, these tiny lines are sometimes known as the Medical Stigmata. For a young person in whose hand these marks are to be seen, one can safely predict a successful career in the medical and caring professions. In a non-practical sensitive hand, however, the likelihood is that the objects of concern, the 'children', will prove to be of a more abstract nature, entailing a practical concern with works of art and personal creations of a similar nature. The Marks of Concern appear in figures 38B and 39B.

A distinctive sign of psychic sensitivity is the Grand Cross, which is occasionally to be seen in the upper part of the palm between the Heart and the Head Lines. This area, between these two major lines, is known as the Great Quadrangle, or the Supernal Zone. This symbolic zone between the twin functions of thinking and feeling represents the mysterious 'void' in which the world of spirit is said to be open to awareness. When thinking and feeling are both still, consciousness should rest within this area, and the palm of the hand may indicate the way in which a hint of this consciousness could arrive.

A cross tends to be a negative sign, in the sense that it expresses opposition to a principle, and to a certain extent may overrule it. Beneath the Mount of Saturn it is called the Mystic

SYMPATHY AND SENSITIVITY

Cross, and implies that the restrictions of Saturn, the influences of materiality and death, are to some extent lifted — enabling the wearer of this sign, without being misled by the occult, to see beyond what is physically obvious. To this extent it implies that its wearer possesses psychic gifts, or partial access to some aspect of spirituality (see figure 38A).

When the Grand Cross appears beneath the Mount of Jupiter, by negating the abstract power of that 'planet', it implies an inner ability to acquire material wealth, a gift for manipulating the money market. It has been called the 'Gambler's Cross', because its wearer always seems to know exactly where to place the bet in order to get results. Finally, when the Grand Cross appears at the opposite end of the palm, beneath the Mount of Mercury, or midway between that mount and the Mount of the Sun, it implies that its wearer will be aware of the negative, mythical side of culture, and its communication. In this position it is known as the 'Occult Cross'. The occult is the abstract side of materiality, the supernatural without spiritual content, and these mysterious things can become an obsession with the wearer of this sign.

The Heart Line, as we have already seen, may curve up and around the Mount of Mercury at its termination, and this is always taken as a mark of sensitivity. Compassion, too, is suggested by a major fork from the Head Line, travelling straight across the palm to meet the Heart Line, usually beneath the Mount of the Sun. But, almost as a development of this link, another feature can arise from within the Supernal Zone (the area between the Heart and Head Line), and this is the Supernal Line (figure 38D). It looks similar to a straight fork from either the Heart or the Head Line, but is attached to neither. It represents exactly that tranquil awareness that exists between thinking and feeling, and its presence implies that its wearer will experience this, the unwilled consciousness of the innermost being. It has its negative side, however, for spiritual understanding is not really compatible with worldly success. The owner of this line, always being able to see opposing viewpoints, will find it difficult to come to a decision, or win an argument, forever seeking a compromise.

13
INFLUENCE AND DOMINANCE

Lines of Influence

In the palm of a complex person, minor Lines of Influence often form an apparently baffling network of fine lines, tying, crossing and intersecting, symbolically carrying the influence of one area of human experience to another, the ongoing process of living a full life, affecting both the conscious workings of heart and mind, and the unconscious happenings of fate. They can also be seen as representing actual people who have most influenced the subject during the course of their life.

To give an accurate reading, it is not usually necessary to commit details and shades of possible meaning to memory as though they represented hard and fast rules. It is usually enough to recall the general significance of the mounts from which they spring, and the function of the line which they approach. They fall broadly into two categories: those which arise from the sphere of home and family, represented by the Mount of Venus, and those which arise from outside the family, represented by the Mount of the Moon (see figure 40A).

If the subject has a Line of Fate, this can be taken to represent the personal self. If you are reading your own palm and you have a Line of Fate, you will probably already have fixed in your mind a timescale to fit it. The age which you have reached is your current Point of Self on this timescale. As an overall view of your life, you will be able to picture your Point of Self as it leaves the Rascette at birth, and climbs slowly up this line as your life

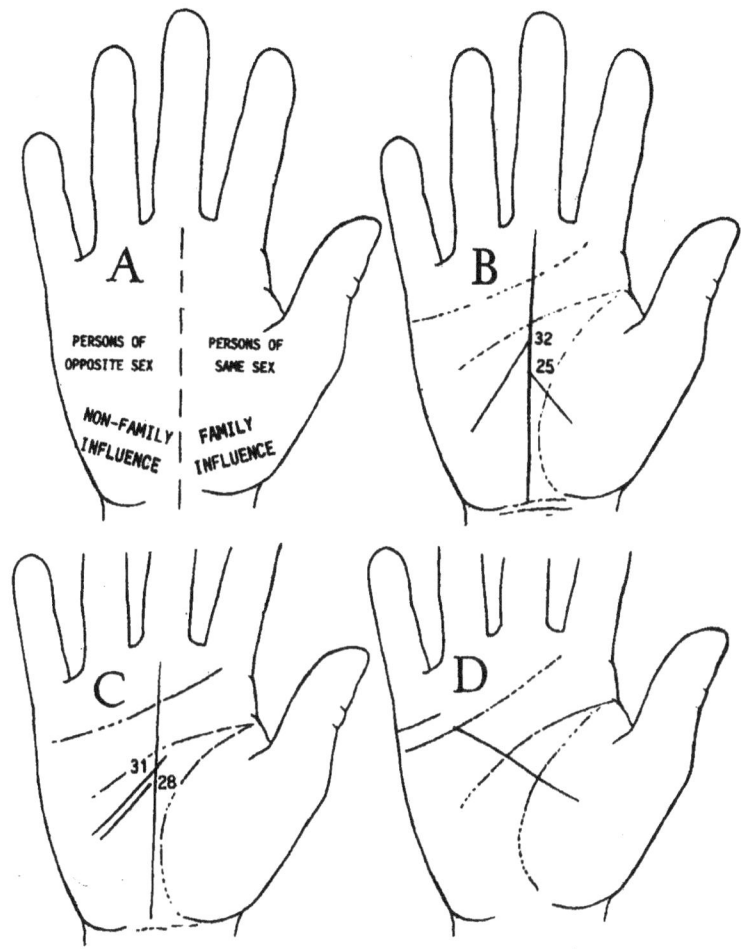

Figure 40
Lines of Influence: (A) possible sources of influence from either side of the Line of Fate; (B) family support arriving at age 25, non-family influence or support arriving at age 32; (C) the arrival of potential life-partners (from the Mount of the Moon), one at age 28 (unlikely to endure), one at age 31 (likely to end in quarrels and eventual separation); (D) Line of Influence from the Mount of Venus approaching the Marriage Line, indicating parental interference in the marriage.

progresses. You can also ascribe a Point of Self to the timescale of your Life Line, of course, but it is the Line of Fate (and, if you have one, your Line of Fortune) that chiefly records incoming Lines of Influence.

As your Point of Self passes your teenage years on the Line of Fate, the Lines of Influence which approach it, or cut across it, can take on a gender of their own. Those which cross the Life Line to reach you from the family side can now be said to represent members of your own sex, and the influence they have on you; those reaching the Line of Fate from the Mount of the Moon can represent influential members of the opposite sex. These could represent any person who has or will have a powerful influence on your life and career. The arrival of someone who might prove to be a staunch friend and ally, or a marriage partner in your life — though not necessarily recording the year of marriage itself — frequently shows in the palm as a strong line slanting upwards from the Mount of the Moon, to reach the Line of Fate at the relevant age on the timescale (figure 40A, B).

Note carefully the ending point of any 'opposite sex' Line of Influence which approaches the Line of Fate from the Mount of the Moon. If it touches and unites with the Line of Fate, it reflects a perfect union, and a successful marriage is very likely to follow. If it fails to reach the Line of Fate, though the match may appear at first ideal, things are liable to go wrong and the marriage knot is unlikely to be tied. The affair will remain in the memory as something that 'might have been' — or even perhaps a lucky escape. The Line of Influence that cuts through the Line of Fate is not a very good omen. It signifies marriage, but hints too at quarrels and eventual separation (figure 40C).

We have already noted how the Marriage Lines may be connected with the Mount of Venus in one way or another, and this is never a happy omen for the success of a marriage. Parents or other relatives are not supposed to interfere. Their influence should stop short of anything calculated to affect their grown-up child's married life. A long Line of Influence running from the Mount of Venus to approach the Marriage Line suggests just such a case of unwanted interference (see figure 40D).

INFLUENCE AND DOMINANCE

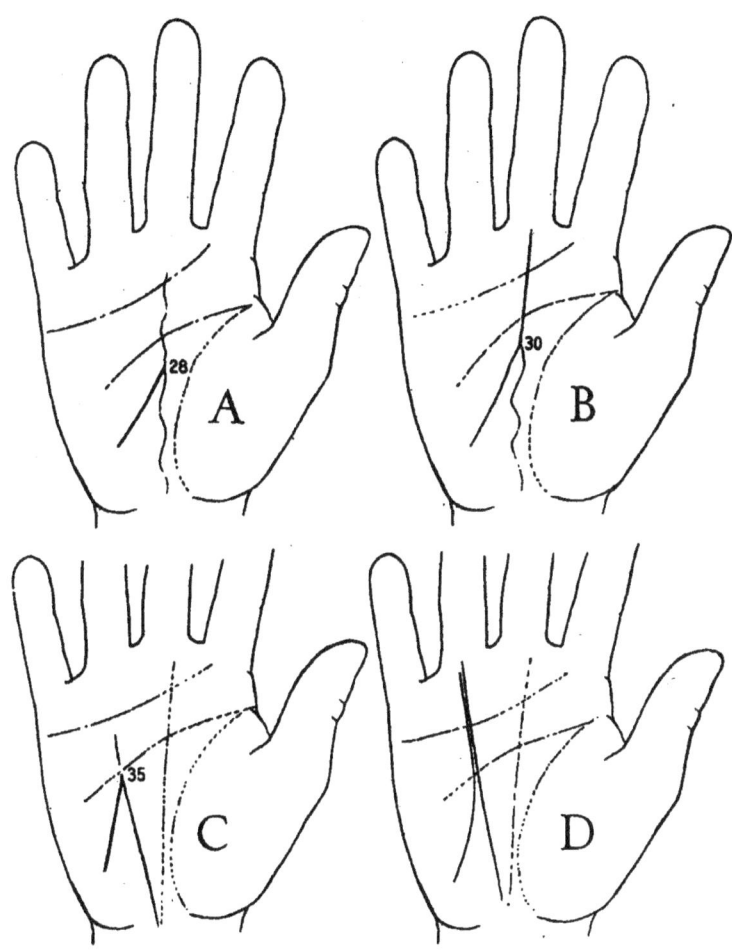

Figure 41
Line of Dominance: (A) dominant partner arriving at the age of 28, followed by a lasting but unsatisfactory arrangement; (B) dominant partner arriving at the age of 30, providing stability and strength to the relationship; (C) dominant business partner arriving (on the Line of Fortune) at the age of 35, resulting in failure and subsequent insecurity; (D) influential partner (from the Mount of the Moon, recorded by the Line of Fortune) adding long-term support to a successful lifestyle.

Lines of Dominance

Dominance is symbolised by the comparative strength of an approaching line. If a Line of Influence is noticeably more strongly marked than the Line of Fate, it may be taken to represent a potentially domineering partner. It then becomes known as a Line of Dominance. There is a big difference between a compatible mate willing to share one's life, playing an equal part — a man's 'better half', a woman's soul-mate — and a prospective partner who wants to carry this complementary process to excess. The sad truth is that many people who fall under the influence of a member of the opposite sex find themselves dominated by them. Not a few end up being constantly nagged, morally crushed and robbed of the most rewarding part of what was meant to be a happy and fulfilling relationship. Of course, the dominant partner may feel that a newfound mate stands in plain need of guidance, and needs moulding into shape. But though we all need a 'pillar of strength' to rely on from time to time, few of us actually want to be controlled (see figure 41A).

Even so, apparent dominance is not always a bad thing. Some people feel the need for a more powerful personality than their own to take over the responsibility of decision-making. You will sometimes see a palm in which an obviously heavy Line of Dominance meets a thin and wavering Line of Fate and, joining up with it, strengthens and straightens it, continuing up the palm beyond the Heart Line. You can be confident that such a relationship will indeed be for the best, and a happy and lasting union can be predicted (see figure 41B).

The Line of Fortune may equally well represent the course of its owner's life, and Lines of Influence which approach or touch it normally carry favourable implications of help in achieving success. As with the Line of Fate, the Mount of Venus should be taken to represent family (and sometimes same-sex) influence, the Mount of the Moon to represent non-family (and sometimes opposite sex) influence. But in this case it is a good name, moral support, or even timely financial help, that is at stake. Possibilities for marriage or physical relationships will not be represented by signs or Lines of Influence to be seen along or in connection with the Line of Fortune (see figure 41C).

There may well be a case of dominance, though, by a business partner or agent, and the comparative strength of these lines should be assessed. A welcome sign of a friendly helping hand is a Line of Influence — whether it arrives from the family Mount of Venus, or the non-family Mount of the Moon — that runs up the palm alongside and close to the Line of Fortune, as though accompanying the Point of Self through its life's journey (see figure 41D).

'He's got an island in his Head Line, and his Fate Line runs out today!'

14
ADVENTURE AND MISADVENTURE

Safe journeys

When someone wants to know what their chances are of success in a particular venture, or, in more general terms, whether they are likely to get the chance to travel widely, and what the results of their travels are likely to be, some of the signs we have already studied can be reinterpreted with these ideas in mind.

The Rascette is a good starting point here. We have already learnt that a chained or islanded topmost bracelet is an indication of minor handicaps and problems to be overcome, and that these may well have the effect of strengthening the resolve and are not really barriers to success and happiness in the long term. But clearly identifiable material success in adventurous undertakings is always more likely to come about when the three bracelets, clearly defined and evenly set, are undisturbed by chains or islands. Although people on whose wrist they are blurred and indistinct, or wavering and broken, may never lack the basic necessities and everyday comforts of life, they cannot realistically expect their enterprises to be resoundingly successful. They are unlikely to become wealthy or famous. But bearing in mind the symbolic nature of these 'barriers' to the normally unconscious dimension which we all share, there may well be compensations in other, less tangible directions. Adventures of the soul may be more rewarding than those of the body, or the brain acting on its own.

Traditionally, when several short lines are to be seen, connecting the topmost bracelet with the Mount of the Moon,

ADVENTURE AND MISADVENTURE

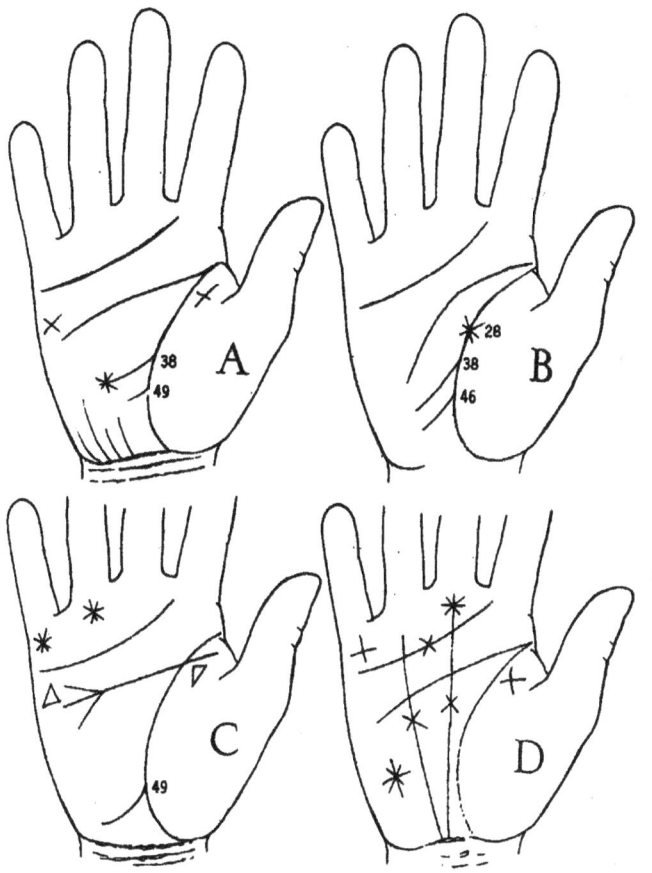

Figure 42
Travel Lines and journeys of the mind: (A) short lines leading from the Rascette to the Mount of the Moon each represents a journey, a star on the Mount of the Moon with a tie from age 38 on the Life Line warns of travel danger, a venture at age 49 may lead to illness, and crosses on the Mounts of Mars warn against aggressive behaviour; (B) a starred Life Line predicts an accident at age 28, followed by journeys of self-discovery at ages 38 and 46; (C) an aggressisve Head Line is mitigated by triangles expressing self-control, a fork suggests broadening of understanding, an important journey at age 49, with optimistic stars on the Mounts of Mercury and the Sun; (D) this hand shows potential difficulties and possible dangers.

corresponding journeys may be predicted (figure 42A). However, as already noted, journeys abroad are so commonplace nowadays that they are unlikely to be recorded in the hand in any literal sense, but instead should be taken to imply completely new and unexpected experiences which prove to have a deep and lasting effect on the subject, so much that they alter the personality and the subject's outlook on life.

On an accident-prone hand, Travel Lines leaving the Life Line can be taken as warnings to take extra care when travelling. These days, the daily routine of driving the children to school is probably more hazardous than flying to the Far East, and one can never be too careful when embarking on everyday journeys. A wide gap between the Head Line and the Life Line at their commencement can portend an ever-present danger of recklessness. This is particularly so when the Head Line then plunges down quite steeply into the Mount of the Moon. Crosses on either of the two Mounts of Mars can be taken as warnings against 'road rage' and aggressive driving (see figure 42A, B).

A break in the Life Line is often interpreted as a risk of accident at that point on the timescale, and stars, too, can have this connotation, particularly on the Life Line and the Line of Fate. The Mount of the Moon is traditionally associated with travel, with oceans, and 'foreign parts' — as the symbol of non-self influences arriving from 'outside' — and a star on this mount should always be taken as a warning against indiscretion or complacency when travelling away from home (see figure 42D).

In the next chapter we shall discuss the difference in significance between the left and the right hands. Where Lines of Travel are concerned, we can now say that the left hand may signify factual, physical journeys; the right hand is more likely to record mental or spiritual journeys of inner discovery. In the case of some people, you will find, the real meaning of this distinction is very plain to see, and they will eagerly give you examples from their experience. But in the case of some others the very concept of a non-material journey is quite meaningless.

Left-handed Lines of Travel usually commence at some point along the Life Line, when they are subject to the Life Line timescale, and head outwards for varying distances. Some hands show an intricate network of such lines, and it could be a major task trying to identify each one and give it a date. You will certainly find it far easier to do this at leisure with your own hand, rather than attempting it for someone else.

On either hand, there is very frequently a curving line which leaves the Life Line at some time during the subject's forties on the timescale, and whilst it may well coincide with some particular journey, it is far more likely to refer to that inward journey of self-discovery and reorientation that most people experience at that time in their lives. Women will have reached that highly significant and sometimes traumatic hurdle, the 'change of life', and men, too, are said to be at 'a funny age' in their middle years, simply by following their normal seven-year cycle. For the individual on whom this experience has a deep impact, the fact will certainly be recorded in their hand (see figure 42C).

A line at this point on the Life Line is more likely to be an actual Travel Line, usually implying emigration, when it features on both hands. If such a line grows stronger than the Life Line, which for its own part tends to fade away as it rounds the Mount of Venus, the implication is that the subject is likely to settle abroad, and not wish to return. In effect, the Travel Line will have taken over the function of the Life Line itself.

Warning signs

A triangle is the symbol of intellect, or mind-control, and when it appears it will mitigate what may otherwise have seemed dangerous or reckless characteristics displayed in the hand. It can hint at adventures of a beneficial kind. The aggressive Head Line that commences below the Life Line, for instance, is a warning of possible unpleasantness, but a triangle on the Lower Mount of Mars offers reassurance that these belligerent instincts will be used intelligently. Another triangle at the Upper Mount of Mars, the abstract seat of tenacity and determination, will balance potential aggression perfectly. The result is likely to be a willingness 'to boldly go' and make the most of dangerous experiences and exciting opportunities — a real adventurer's sign (see figure 42C).

Remember, too, the significance of small forks running from the Head Line, symbolising the brain which loves to explore every available possibility. People who are adventurous both in the physical and especially the mental sphere, often bear several small forks at the end of their Head Line, demonstrating their willingness to experiment, extending their interests in all directions. If the subject has a Line of Fortune, a small Head Line fork adjoining this line signifies a major business venture that will be successful provided the fork does not actually cut through the line of Fortune: a narrow line, that is, between outstanding success and resounding disaster!

To summarise, signs of potential success are: Stars, particularly when they appear on the Mounts of the Sun and Mercury; on the Line of Fortune, adjacent to but not actually on the Line of Fate, and on the Rascette. Squares, don't forget, are always reassuring signs wherever they appear, seeming to cancel out potential dangers indicated by other signs. Triangles are also encouraging, because they indicate an innate ability to apply intellectual solutions to any problems that arise.

Signs of potential risks and difficulties are: Stars, when they appear on the Mounts of Saturn and the Moon, and on the two Mounts of Mars — stars, of course, symbolise an increase in the factors suggested by the lines, in this case, respectively, of over-concern with the material things of life, of woolly-mindedness, and of aggression; similarly, when stars feature on the Head Line, Life Line and Line of Fate (though they can predict material gain when they appear alongside but not actually on the Line of Fate). Crosses are warning signs, particularly when they appear on the Mounts of Saturn and the Moon; on the Mount of Mercury when reliance is being placed on others; on the two mounts of Mars; also when they appear on the Heart Line, the Line of Fate and the Line of Fortune. Islands are also warning signs, but they relate chiefly to psychological rather than physical dangers, as do chained formations. Crossbars are warning signs to the adventurer when they appear on the Lines of Fate and Fortune, and breaks are also warnings, especially when they appear on the Lines of Fate and Fortune.

15
LEFT HAND — RIGHT HAND

Inheritance

To follow the full course of a person's life so as to obtain a complete picture of their developing character, you really need to study both hands placed side by side. Read them from left to right, like a book, and together they will tell an ongoing saga. The left hand shows characteristics that are inherited or inborn — the traits that are our own at the beginning, as a child, before we begin to shed or at least to modify early parental influence. The right hand shows how we develop, and what we are able to make of these inherited characteristics as we get older. Having read and understood the basics of palmistry, now is the time to study this variation between the hands. You will appreciate that it can only be fully interpreted when the basic principles of each line, and the meanings attached to each sign, are themselves fully understood.

If there is little or no difference between somebody's left and right hands, we assume that, essentially, they are much the same in adulthood as they were as children. They will have matured and developed in many ways, of course, but they will not have developed any extra qualities beyond their inherited lot. Equally, they will not have wasted any quality, or allowed any inherited talent to diminish.

People who have endured a difficult time as a child may need to work particularly hard in later life to overcome their early disadvantages, striking out during adolescence to develop independence of thought, cultivating a determination to succeed. They may

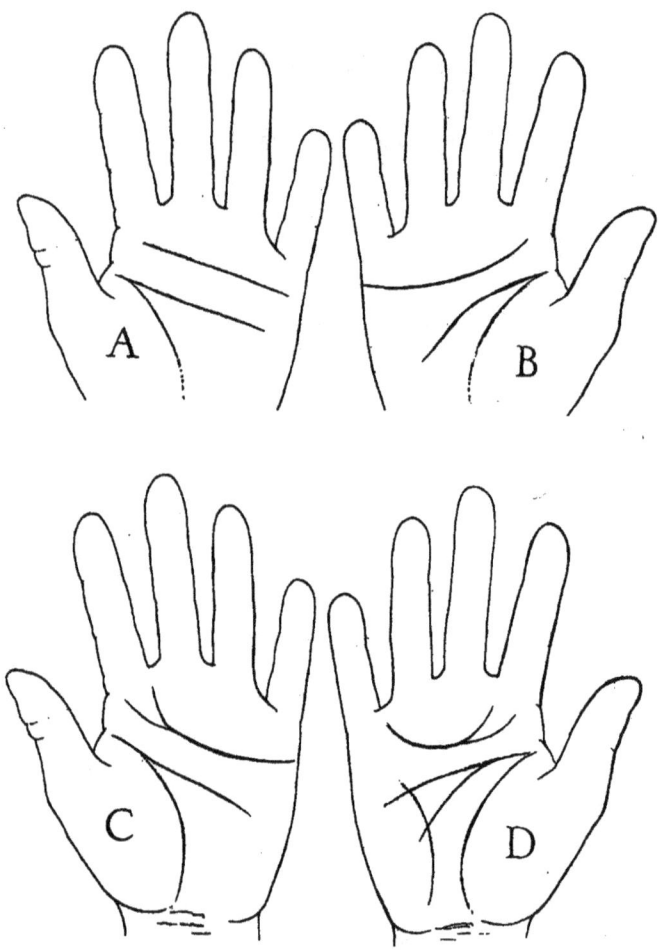

Figure 43
Left hand — right hand: (A) straight Head and Heart Lines on the left hand give way to (B) curved versions on the right; (C) an inherited long and curving Heart Line gives way to (D) a curtailed version enclosing the Mount of the Sun; the Head Line has acquired an exploratory fork, and a Line of Intuition suggests that this faculty has been developed during adulthood.

feel the need to make the most of what they have, in the most practical way; or they may simply feel relief at having escaped early duties and responsibilities, let their studies slip along with their early promise, waste their potential and never bother to use their mental capacity to its full extent. Upgraded or downgraded, all this will show in the difference between their left and their right hands.

Very often a distinctive feature in a parent's right hand, such as a Head Line to Heart Line link, perhaps the result of their own early experiences and their reactions to these experiences, will make its appearance in the child's left hand; it has become part of their inheritance. They in turn may well modify the characteristic further as a response to their own early experiences, so their right hand may again show quite a different pattern. The right hand, in other words, will indicate an individual psychic response to inherited characteristics.

Commonly seen examples will include a straight left-handed Heart Line which has become curved in the right hand (figure 43A-B), suggesting that an emotionally starved upbringing may have triggered a need for giving and receiving emotional warmth. Or a generously long, curving Heart Line in the left hand may have become curtailed in the right, surrounding the Mount of the Sun instead of the Mount of Mercury (figure 43C-D). The implication is that unpleasant experiences during adolescence have taught that individual to keep their feelings and natural emotional responses strictly to themselves; to decide to grin and bear it rather than complain when faced with less than perfect prospects of adulthood. Again, a plunging, easy-going Head Line in the left hand may give way to a straight, no-nonsense version in the right hand, hinting at a youthful determination to improve their inherited lot, and work hard at the very things in which their parents had no interest or aptitude.

Similarly, the rising point of a Head Line, and the extent to which it is tied or free from the Life Line, often — or usually — varies between left and right, as the experiences of childhood give a young person the capacity or need for more, or less, independence than his or her original birthright would have suggested. Thus a particularly wide gap between Head Line and

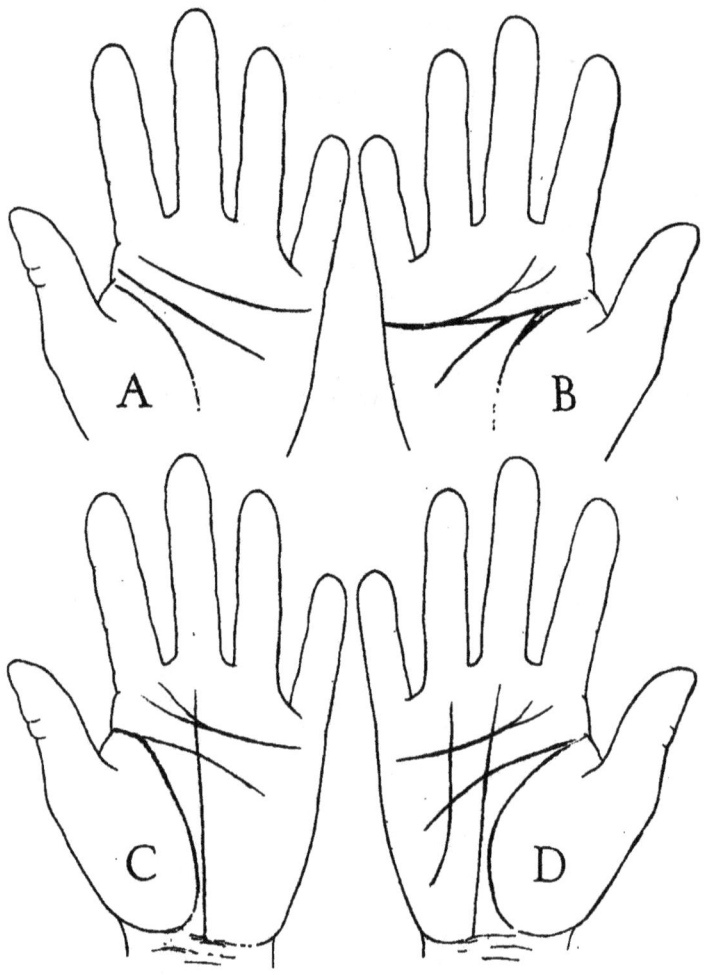

Figure 44
Left hand — right hand: (A) an apparently straightforward and confident attitude has given way to (B) a shy approach to life, indicated by the extensive Head to Life Line tie, and the development of the emotional quality of compassion is indicated by the straight Head Line to Heart Line branch; (C) a promising inheritance has acquired (D) a Line of Fortune rising from outside the family, resulting in an eminently successful career.

Life Line in the left hand, whilst promising a bold and energetic approach to life and hinting at physical bravery, which gives way to a less pronounced gap on the right hand, will suggest that the subject has been obliged to 'draw in his horns' to some extent, as the result of some early setback (figure 44A-B).

When the differences are very pronounced, the switch-over from left to right-handed features normally takes place at a definite time in the subject's life. This change often occurs at one of the seven-year 'hurdles' — usually at the age of 28, but quite often seven years later, at 35. A young person reading his or her own hand, should use the left-handed pattern to depict their current situation. Their right hand will show what can, or will, come to pass, if they recognise their natural instincts and follow their own independent spirit when they attain the age, let us say, of 28 years.

Material and abstract

Even without taking inheritance into consideration, and ignoring the psychological changes that should take place at the crucial time, either hand should give an accurate sketch of the personality, but with subtle differences. If we say that the left hand indicates the practical, material realities of life, and the right hand the more abstract, intellectual and spiritual possibilities, you will see that this analysis amounts to more or less the same thing. The left hand equates to the essential raw ingredients of a life; the right hand holds out the promise of creative possibilities open to the individual, like the tempting illustrations in a cook-book.

Features that are the same in both hands should always be taken to refer to hard and fast characteristics or occurrences that may be kept hidden or glossed over by the subject, but they cannot be altered. Such features are stressed or confirmed by this duplication. However, it often happens that a Line of Intuition may appear on the right hand only, expressing conscious development of intuitive powers, and the constructive use of an increasingly powerful imagination (figure 43D); or a Line of Fortune may make its appearance on the right hand, as a promise of non-material success to come (figure 44D).

16
SUMMARY OF HUMAN CHARACTERISTICS

Aggression

We all get annoyed. Even quite refined and respectable people can become aggressive at times. Circumstances can build up until eventually we lose our tempers. Some individuals, however, are basically confrontational; aggression is their staff of life. They may find a useful outlet in the martial arts, boxing or wrestling. Such are the anomalies of fate, however, that some of the most aggressive people are often physically small, and female.

The Lower Mount of Mars is the seat of aggression, and this will be particularly well developed. With the owner of a rugged type of hand, an aggressive nature is perhaps to be expected, but the surest give-away is the clubbed thumb, which may sometimes be seen on small and otherwise quite delicate hands.

The Heart Line in an aggressive hand will be well defined, but often short. Most significantly the Head Line occasionally rises beneath the Life Line, on the Lower Mount of Mars itself. If it then runs straight across the palm, common sense is likely to prevail during confrontational situations; if it plunges down into the Mount of the Moon, however, extreme aggression is to be expected. Alternatively, the Life Line may rise from a lower point than average, also on the Lower Mount of Mars, as if to colour that individual's life with physically confrontational urges. The Line of Fate will usually be present and strongly defined, and the Mount of Saturn above it may bear a cross — a warning symbol of the most dangerous and often self-destructive kind of aggression (figure 45).

SUMMARY OF HUMAN CHARACTERISTICS

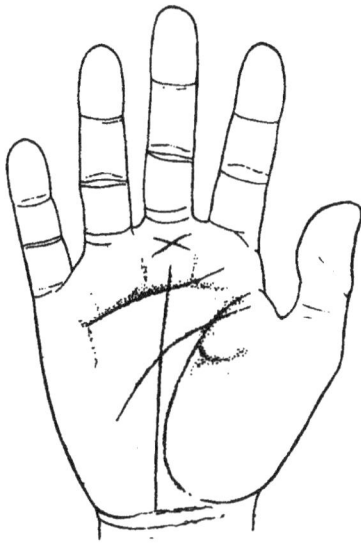

Figure 45

An aggressive hand

Ambition

We have seen that the Mount of Jupiter is the seat of ambition, and in the hand of an ambitious person it is bound to be well developed and prominent. From this point, symbolically, ambition is radiated over the palm and channelled along the main streams of energy. The Heart Line in particular will have this mount as its rising point, and from there it will run fully across the palm, often curving upwards at its termination, cutting across the Mount of Mercury, the seat of business and social influence. A strong Jupiter Heart Line will represent an emotional desire to succeed not only in these fields, however, but also in the kind of prestige and cultural advancement represented by the Mount of the Sun, and in the pursuit of wealth and property reflected by the Mount of Saturn.

The Head Line and Life Line, too, will start high, at the base of the Mount of Jupiter. Alternatively, they may bear an early tieline connecting them to this mount. The Line of Fate, if present, is sure also to bear some kind of connection with the Mount of Jupiter, sometimes even diverting its course away from its usual destination on the Mount of Saturn, to reach the base of the index finger. There will probably be a fairly wide gap between the Head and the Life Lines at their commencement, indicating the independence of spirit necessary to venture and succeed. The index finger will be longer than average, and all the fingers are likely to be broad, supple, and smoothly knuckled (figure 46).

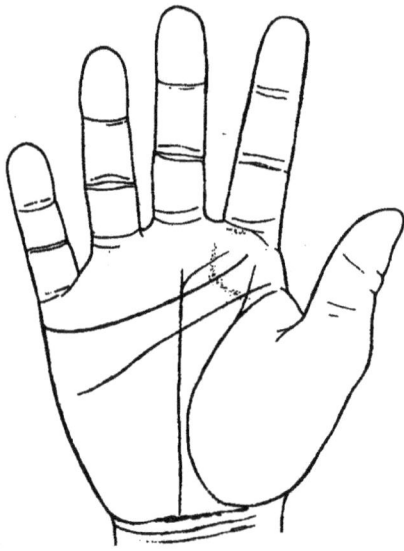

Figure 46

An ambitious hand

Assertiveness

This is a type of modified aggression that finds a socially acceptable, intelligent and logically thought-out goal — usually some kind of dominance over other people. Assertive characters may possess an aggressive Head Line, commencing below the Life

Line on the Lower Mount of Mars. The wearer of such a Head Line will be tenacious in pursuing his or her ends, whether in politics or society. The topmost bracelet of the Rascette will be chained or islanded, indicating stubborn persistence. The Mount of Jupiter is likely to carry the sign of the grid on the hand of those who seek to dominate others. If the Line of Fate is present, it will probably be clearly defined but wavering along its course. The index finger is likely to be as long as the second finger, and the thumb will also be proportionately long.

Creativity

The area of the palm relating to this most human of virtues is the Mount of the Moon. As we saw in earlier chapters, this large mount occupies the quarter of the palm representing all in human nature that is abstract and 'non-self' in origin. Creativity requires an element of adventure and risk-taking, a willingness to stand alone and follow tracks that are not generally trod. When the hand is at rest, the little finger will seem noticeably more widely separated than the other fingers, indicating a preference for the unconventional. The Head Line will be barely, if at all, tied to the Life Line at its commencement, reflecting bold independence. The Head Line will then dip down quite deeply into the Mount of the Moon, with or without a straight fork-prong running across the palm as though to balance logical calculation with abstract ideas.

Creative thoughts have two ways of reaching awareness — through the conscious mental process (via the Head Line), and through the faculty of intuition (via the Line of Intuition). A creative idea can be seen as a two-way process, a circuit perhaps, between the seat of awareness — that is, the Mount of Jupiter — and the seat of logical valuation — the Mount of Mercury — via the abstract 'pool' of imaginative thought — the Mount of the Moon. When this circuit is complete, the idea can be given practical application. Intuitive ideas and flashes of understanding which are not put to practical use may be fascinating, but, by definition, true creativity implies action and purpose.

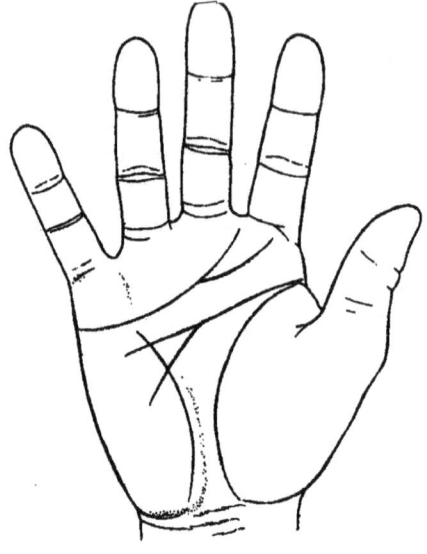

Figure 47

A creative hand

Depression

We all know it as a temporary setback. A bout of depression can appear and just as quickly disappear in all of us; but in some people it can be life-threateningly severe. A congenitally depressive personality often seems to accompany the 'pyknic' type of physique: thickset, short-limbed, and with fairly small but broad hands. The Mount of Saturn is traditionally said to be the seat of depression, as the factor of mortality and limitation. In the hand of a chronically depressed person, the Heart Line often rises solely on this mount. In cases where the Heart Line rises with equal tributaries on both the Mount of Saturn and the Mount of Jupiter, without other modifying tributaries, you may find tendencies towards bipolar disorder, with powerful moods alternating between the extremes of depression and elation. When the Head Line is strongly tied to the Life Line at its outset and then plunges quite deeply down the palm, the subject may well suffer periodically

SUMMARY OF HUMAN CHARACTERISTICS

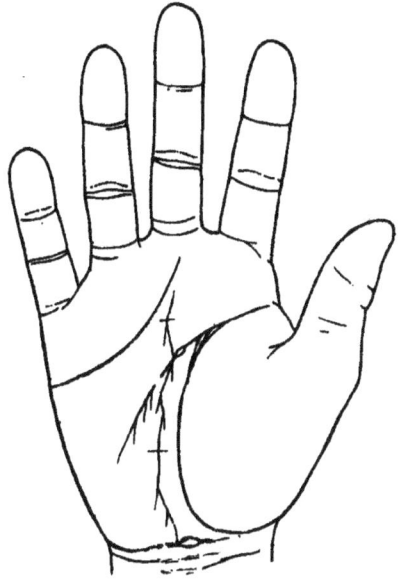

Figure 48

A depressive hand

from a frustrating feeling of purposelessness, a type of habitual pessimism. Even when the Head Line does not slope, and is not too closely tied to the Life Line, an island on the Head Line beneath the Mount of Saturn will suggest an isolated but severe and possibly protracted bout of depression. If such an island also occurs along the Life Line, the diagnosis is fairly certain. There may be minor tielines connecting a Head Line island with the Line of Fate or the Life Line, when the timescales of either of these two lines may be used to foretell the subject's age at the time of the attack. A clean break in the Head Line may also be taken as an indication of recurring depression. A crossbar on the Line of Fate again will hint at an isolated period of deep depression, and this too may be dated with a timescale. Where there are many small lines running downwards from both the Head Line and the Line of Fate, these inevitably carry with them the idea of depression, of negative impulses, a feeling of hopelessness, a draining away of psychic energy and confidence (see figure 48).

Faithfulness

A branch line rising from the Head Line and connecting with the Heart Line at their commencement, implies that the wearer will be faithful and true to his or her partner throughout life, and be of unstinting help in all matters of partnership, whether domestic, social or business. The Mount of Venus is the seat of romance as well as family relationships. Elsewhere on the hand, a cross normally symbolises some kind of threat or outside interference, but where the Mount of Venus is concerned, a cross can be taken as an assurance that he or she is likely to remain loyally attached to one lover, or close partner, in an abiding relationship. If there is a threat, it will be to others who may try to intrude on this relationship. On the Mount of Jupiter, too, a cross implies a secure marriage. The 'threat' here will be to personal independence of the soul, personal pride, personal ambitions. All such possibilities will be sacrificed unselfishly to the success of the partnership. The Marriage Line that curves upwards into the Mount of the Sun implies a steady, happy relationship, so too when this line meets the Line of Fortune — provided it does not cut through this line and set its course instead towards the Saturnian mount of material gain.

Fickleness

This is an emotional problem, and both Heart Line and Mount of Venus will provide clues to this aspect of personality. In the hand of a fickle person the Heart Line, which is likely to have risen with equal tributaries on the Mounts of Jupiter and Saturn, will usually be chained along part of its length. This configuration symbolises emotions, or emotional attachments, that seem unable to run straight and true, but swirl unexpectedly this way and that — all quite without any malicious intention. Feelings of affection will be completely unpredictable. Even apparently sincere assurances of true love will quickly prove unreliable. Beaks in the Heart Line, too, can predict abrupt changes in emotional direction, or possibly

SUMMARY OF HUMAN CHARACTERISTICS

a baffling withdrawal of affection which will certainly be interpreted by abandoned partners as fickleness or inconstancy. If a Line of Fate is present in the hand of an incorrigibly fickle person, it may be strong and deeply defined, but it will pursue a wavering course throughout its length. The Mount of Venus will be prominent and appear well developed, but it will prove soft and yielding to the touch. It will very likely bear several pronounced lines radiating from the thumb and reaching as far as the Life Line, each line representing to the palmist a separate 'love' in the subject's life.

Look out, too, for the doubling up of lines, in particular the Line of Fate and the Marriage Line (see chapter 10), for this characteristic is strongly suggestive of duplicity in matters of romance. The Marriage Line, too, may curve upwards around the Mount of Mercury, implying that the true feelings of its owner are certain not to be made known to the official partner of the moment. The Mount of Mercury, too, will probably seem particularly prominent, and if the Heart Line bears an island below this mount, or a series of breaks close to the edge of the hand, guilty secrets and liaisons are likely to be a recurring problem.

Introspection

We may notice that some people seem to project outwards all the feelings they have about any of their experiences, so that nothing seems to affect them too deeply. Others seem to take all the feelings they experience deep inside themselves, as though to retain and evaluate them on a personal basis. The immediate effect of this is to make the first kind of person seem 'outgoing', reacting quickly to social situations, and interacting readily with others, while remaining largely untouched by deep emotions or misgivings.

The second type of person by contrast seems comparatively slow to react in social situations, and may be thought somewhat withdrawn, 'uninvolved', or even self-absorbed. This apparent absorption is the result of introspection. It is not a selfish trait and, indeed, a certain amount of it is essential to us if we wish to know and understand our own selves. The Upper Girdle of Venus provides a sure sign of a character capable of introspection. He or she is liable to experience emotions at a deeper and more personal level than most others. To strengthen this trait, the Head Line will tend to dip deeply into the Mount of the Moon.

Excessive introspection can lead to, or at least be associated with, mental unbalance and psychological isolation. One token of this danger is an island on the Head Line beneath the Mount of Saturn. There may also be a grid formation on this mount. In most people such excesses tend to be limited to definite periods marked by seven-year and twenty-eight-year cycles. Other indications being absent, the palmist may fairly confidently predict relief from the type of suffering caused by excessive introspection, particularly at the age of 28 or 56, depending upon their current age.

Jealousy

In a jealous hand, the Heart Line will probably rise on the Mount of Saturn, implying that the flow of emotions will always have a flavour of possessive materiality. The Heart Line will be strongly defined, long and straight, high on the palm as though constricting the objective mounts. A jealous person is often fiercely passionate, and the Mount of Venus will be prominent, well developed, and firm to the touch. A triangle on the Mount of Venus will imply that those feelings associated with intimate relationships are liable to come under the scrutiny of logic — which is not quite the same as the power of reason. In this sphere, logical, calculating thoughts tend to lead to suspicion, mistrust and jealousy in love or marriage. The Mounts of Jupiter and Saturn may both bear a grid formation, as though to taint the flow of emotions with negative feelings of distrust. The Line of Fate, if present, is likely to bear a chain formation, and the timescale may be applied to predict the period of maximum disruption.

The Line of Fate may very likely rise on or within the Life Line, indicating that the root cause of this negativity arose from

SUMMARY OF HUMAN CHARACTERISTICS

early experiences within the family circle. An island low down on the Line of Fate will carry a similar meaning — an emotional disruption during childhood (see figure 49).

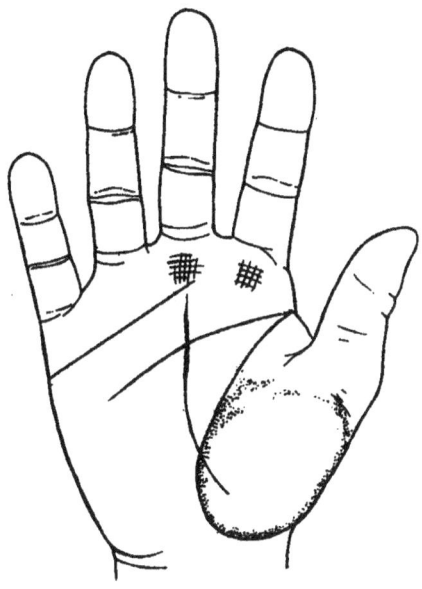

Figure 49

A jealous hand

Kindness

Caring about others is an emotional quality, and signs of it are to be sought in the Heart Line, particularly one which culminates on the Mount of Mercury — the seat of compassion. Kindness within the family circle, however, is not always quite the same thing, particularly when it appears to exclude outsiders. In this case its signs are likely to be found within the Life Line, on the Mount of Venus. A kind person tends to transfer his or her impressions about another person or, as it may be, another creature, from the psychic compartment of 'thoughts' to that of 'feelings', to be acted upon within the emotional sphere. In the hand, as a token of this, there is likely to be a branch line running from the Head Line to meet the Heart Line. Typically kindness, as a first and natural reaction to circumstances, is represented by a branch of this type which leaves the Head Line beneath the material-factual Mount of Saturn, and joins the Heart Line beneath the communicative-compassionate Mount of Mercury. It tends thus to form a straight line across the palm, and the Heart Line as it nears the edge of the palm will then seem particularly deep and strongly defined, doubled up or reinforced. The type of kindness that tends to limit itself to the family circle, usually implying a certain degree of self-sacrifice for the sake of the other family members, can be inferred from the 'Setting Star of Venus' — a clearly marked star set low down on the Mount of Venus, near the wrist.

Moodiness

This temperamental, unpredictable characteristic is mainly a matter for the emotions, expressed through the Heart Line, and implies an inbuilt tendency, in effect, to switch without warning from one emotional track to another. The Heart Line that rises with equal tributaries from the Mounts of Jupiter and Saturn is entirely typical of this trait. There will be no middle ground of compromise which could be symbolised by a tributary rising between the mounts. The difference between the two emotional currents is the difference, basically, between hope and experience, between the ambitions of Jupiter and the material realities of Saturn. Moodiness could be said to represent a mild form of recurrent depression, and it very often accompanies the thickset, bull-necked, pyknic type of physique, typified by fairly small but broad, strong hands. A 'mood' can also suggest a break in the smooth flow of energy, whether that flow is directed along emotional, mental or physical lines. Reflecting this, it can be symbolised by a break — usually an overlapping break — in any of the three major lines. Commonly, the Heart Line in particular will show an overlapping break beneath the Mount of the Sun. The normally unconscious 'inner feelings' may also be involved in unexplained and seemingly unex-

SUMMARY OF HUMAN CHARACTERISTICS

plainable mood swings, and the Upper Girdle of Venus will very likely be clearly defined. A sudden 'mood' may be the outward sign of a feeling that one's personal inegrity, one's unspoken quest for wholeness, is being threatened, from whatever outward cause. The onset of moodiness therefore may occur at any time, and in unpredictable circumstances (see figure 50).

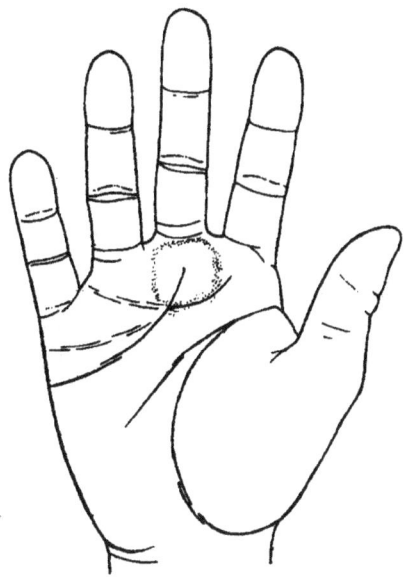

Figure 50

A moody hand

Resourcefulness

Symbolising corporeal existence, the Mount of Saturn is the seat of material resources as they influence the personality, and reflects the way in which they are habitually managed. In a resourceful person's hand this mount is sure to be well developed, but it should not bear any minor signs other than a triangle or, possibly, a square. The Heart Line will certainly have a major tributary from the

Mount of Saturn, although it is unlikely to rise exclusively on it; the Mount of Jupiter is sure to be strongly involved too. This will imply that the necessary flow of ambition, of determination, is always available. The middle ground between the mounts will probably also provide a tributary as if to maintain a smooth, even balance between two emotional extremes. The shape of the hand itself will be within the practical range, the set of the fingers evenly disposed so that they are almost level.

The three major lines will be long and clearly defined. The Head Line will cross the palm fairly high, and possibly even curve upwards at the end, towards the Mount of Mercury. There will very likely be a link or a more definite branch line running from the Heart Line near its commencement to the Head Line, in such a way that the Mount of Saturn is closely involved. The implication is that when a solution to material problems is needed, emotional matters will be delegated to the process of logic. The Head Line may bear a broad, even fork, so as to touch the Mounts of Upper Mars and the Moon, making full use of logical reasoning and of more imaginative, creative solutions to any problem (figure 51).

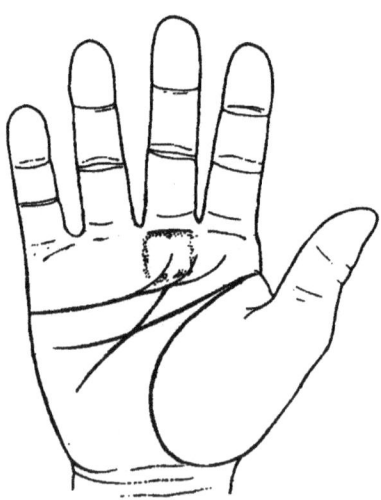

Figure 51

A resourceful hand

SUMMARY OF HUMAN CHARACTERISTICS

Self-confidence

Inwardly and outwardly, there are two types of self-confidence: confidence in one's ability to deal with things and events; and the ability to be at ease with all sorts of people. Some lives seem to be mapped out very clearly, and these individuals will be found to entertain very few self-doubts in any situation. This characteristic is symbolised by the Line of Fate, which will be clearly defined, comparatively unmarked, straight and long, reaching from the uppermost bracelet to the Mount of Saturn. A noticeably self-confident person will probably have the small, neat hands and smooth knuckles of one who can move easily in society. All their main lines will be well proportioned and clearly defined. The uppermost bracelet of the Rascette may well be chained, however, suggesting an innate ability to tackle and solve everyday problems with ease. There is sure to be at least a slight gap between the Head and the Life Lines at their commencement — on the right hand, at least. There need be no cautious clinging to inherited safeguards such as a tied Head Line might suggest, or the slightest dependence on the opinions of others. Such a person will not even begin to entertain self-doubts.

'No... that's not right ... I'm not negative ... not me ... no way.'

17
SUMMARY OF VOCATIONAL SIGNS

Accountant

The accountant's thumb should be straight and full-waisted. Heart Line rising on, or with strong tributary from, the Mount of Saturn. Head Line fairly straight and long. Line of Fate an advantage only when clearly defined and straight. Well-developed Mounts of Saturn and Upper Mars. Triangles are advantageous, particularly when appearing along the Line of Fate or on the upper mounts.

Actor

The performer's Heart Line will rise on, or with a strong tributary from, the Mount of Jupiter, long, fairly deep and curving. Head Line sloping to the top of the Mount of the Moon. A clean Line of Fate is good, but a well-developed Line of Fortune is essential for real success, ideally one that is starred and runs clearly to the Mount of the Sun. The topmost bracelet may be chained or islanded. The Mounts of Jupiter, Sun, Mercury, Upper Mars and Moon should all be well developed.

Architect

The architect's hand should have equal tributaries from the Mounts of Jupiter and Saturn, afterwards running clear and long, leading to the Mount of Mercury. Head Line should run fairly straight across

SUMMARY OF VOCATIONAL SIGNS

the palm or be evenly forked, with the topmost fork straight. A Line of Intuition would be a great advantage. Well-developed mounts, especially the Mount of Mercury.

Artist

The cheirotype will probably be in the artistic to practical range, differentiating between fine artwork, such as painting, and the more manipulatory, manual kinds, such as sculpture. Heart Line often deeply curved and usually long. Upper Girdle of Venus, especially the open variety, is an advantage. Head Line should reach to the Mount of the Moon. Line of Intuition is often present. Well-developed mounts, especially the Mount of Mercury.

Athlete

Most likely a firm, squarish hand, with fairly straight thumbs and strong, fairly stiff fingers. Strong, clear lines, especially the Life Line; an Inner Life Line is a great advantage. Heart Line closely associated with the Mount of Jupiter, often carrying a branch to the Head Line, which should be fairly straight. Usually a pronounced gap between Head and Life Lines at their commencement. There will be few minor links. The topmost bracelet is often chained or islanded. Well-developed Mounts of Mars.

Banker

This will be a firm hand with clear major lines. Fingerprints probably whorled. Heart Line associated with the Mount of Saturn, fairly straight and long. Head Line also fairly straight. A clear Line of Fate is an advantage. Well-developed mounts, especially Jupiter, Saturn and Mercury. A cross beneath the Mount of Jupiter suggests skill with money dealings.

Builder

Showing practical hands and fingers. Heart Line should bear equal tributaries from Mounts of Saturn and Jupiter. Head Line should run fairly straight across the palm. The Life Line should be strong and clear. Squares anywhere on the hand are a very auspicious sign. Triangles are also good, especially on the Line of Fate, which should be well developed. Strongly developed Mounts are essential, especially the four uppermost, and both Upper and Lower Mars.

Chemist

A chemist's fingers are typically long, the thumbs fairly long and supple. Heart Line should rise between the Mounts of Jupiter and Saturn, or with equal tributaries, travelling fairly low across the palm and curving upwards at the end. Head Line is best lightly tied to the Life Line, and long, reaching beneath the Mount of Mercury. The Life Line should be strongly defined. Upper mounts well developed.

Church minister

The Heart Line should be seen to rise clearly on the Mount of Jupiter with a tributary from between the mounts, long and fairly deeply curved, outlining the Mount of Mercury at its termination. The Head Line is often forked, or dipping into the upper parts of the Mount of the Moon. A Line of Intuition is an advantage. The Line of Sympathy, the Upper Girdle of Venus and the Marks of Concern, if present, all show desirable characteristics. The Rascette is often fragmented. Well-developed Mounts of Jupiter, Sun, Mercury, Moon and Venus.

SUMMARY OF VOCATIONAL SIGNS

Clerical officer

Office management favours a long and straight Heart Line with equal tributaries from the Mounts of Jupiter and Saturn. Head Line fairly straight or evenly forked. There is often a branch from the Heart to the Head Line, which should be loosely tied to the Life Line. Triangles are advantageous, especially on the Mounts of Jupiter, Saturn, Sun and Moon.

Computer programmer

A clear, straight Heart Line should be strongly connected to the Mount of Jupiter, and often branched onto the Head Line, which should be long and gently descending to reach the upper part of the Mount of the Moon. A Line of Fate, if present, should be clear and decisive, reaching the Mount of Saturn. Well developed Mounts of the Moon, Mercury and Upper Mars. Triangles on lines and the Mount of Saturn are advantageous.

Cook

These will be practical hands with well-developed Mounts of Jupiter and Venus. Heart Line rising on, or with strong tributaries from, the Mount of Jupiter, continuing long and deeply curved across the palm. Head Line sloping into the Mount of the Moon. Lines of influence often present, rising from the Mount of Venus to meet the Head and the Heart Lines. The Mount of Venus is often starred near the wrist.

Doctor

A doctor's hands often differ markedly. Typically the left hand bears caring signs: Marks of Concern, Mark of Mercy, also Upper Girdle of Venus and a Head Line to Heart Line link. The right hand is often clear of such signs, the Heart Line usually long and slightly curved, the Head Line, scarcely attached to the Life line, runs fairly straight across the palm. A Line of Intuition is often present and is distinctly beneficial.

Draftsperson

This will be a practical hand with artistic or spatulate fingertips. Clearly defined main lines. Heart Line strongly associated with the Mount of Jupiter and leading to the Mount of Mercury. Head Line fairly straight, or with an evenly disposed lower fork reaching or nearing the Mount of the Moon. Head Line lightly tied to the Life Line. If a Line of Fate is present, it should be clear and straight. Well-developed mounts.

Driver (bus or lorry)

These are likely to be practical hands with strong fingers. Head Line will probably swoop downwards to reach the Mount of the Moon and may bear a fork near its end. The Rascette should be clear and well developed. The uppermost mounts and the Mount of Venus should all be well developed. The Mount of Mercury may bear Marks of Concern, and the Mount of Jupiter and the Life Line are likely to bear a triangle.

Engineer

An engineer's hand should be firm and practical, fingers fairly stiff, thumbs large and fairly long. Heart Line rising on, or heavily tributaried from, the Mount of Saturn, and often has a branch to the Head Line, which should run fairly straight across the palm. If a Line of Fate is present it should be clear and straight. The objective Mounts of Jupiter, Saturn, Sun and Mercury, also both Mounts of Mars and the Mount of Venus, should all be well developed.

SUMMARY OF VOCATIONAL SIGNS

Farmer

A large, practical hand with knobbly fingerjoints. Heart Line rising on the Mount of Jupiter. Head Line typically commencing slightly above the Life Line or only lightly tied to it, dipping to reach the Mount of the Moon, or with a clear fork, the topmost prong running straight across the palm. There is often a branch from the Head to the Heart Line. The Life Line should be clear and long, preferably with an Inner Life Line. Well-developed Mounts, especially of Jupiter, Lower and Upper Mars, and Venus. The central phalange of the Saturn finger is often seen to be longer than the other two.

Fashion designer

Typically, this will be an artistic hand with squarish fingertips. Heart Line rising mainly on the Mount of Jupiter, long and probably deeply curved. Head Line often forked, otherwise reaching into the Mount of the Moon. The Line of Fortune, if present, is a great advantage. Well-developed uppermost Mounts, especially of Jupiter. A triangle is a good sign, especially when on the subjective, little finger side of the hand.

Forester

Typically, hands in the normal to practical range, with knobbly knuckles. Heart Line rising on the Mount of Jupiter and between the mounts, Head Line sloping down to reach the top of the Mount of the Moon, tied for a short distance with the Life Line, which should be clear, deep and unmarked. The Line of Fate is typically present, but often faintly sketched and commencing on the Life Line. The Mounts of Jupiter, Venus, and Upper and Lower Mars will be well developed and firm.

Hospital administrator

Organising managers often have small hands, with long, smoothly knuckled fingers. Heart Line rising usually between the Mounts of Jupiter and Saturn, long and gently curving, often with a branch reaching the Head Line, which typically starts a little way above the Life Line, and runs fairly straight across the palm. Well-developed mounts all round. Triangles are an excellent sign, particularly on the Mount of Mercury. Marks of Concern and the Mark of Mercy will also be advantageous.

Hotel manager

Typically with small, smooth hands. The Heart Line probably rises with tributaries from the Mount of Saturn and between the mounts, running straight. Line of Fate straight and clear. Line of Fortune often present, usually rising on the Mount of the Moon. Life Line often touched by Line of Influence, and with Travel Lines. Triangles portend well, particularly when on the Mount of the Moon and the Heart Line.

Journalist

The Heart Line should rise mainly on the Mount of Jupiter, and typically run long and low, ending on the Mount of Mercury, and with a strong link to the Head Line. Head Line tied for some little way to the Life Line, usually sloping to the upper regions of the Mount of the Moon, but often forked, the top prong running straight across the palm, the other touching the Mount of the Moon. Line of Intuition should be deeply curving. Life Line should be firm and clear. Lower Girdle of Venus and Line of Sympathy and right-handed Travel Lines often present. All the mounts should be well developed. Squares are very beneficial on lines and mounts.

SUMMARY OF VOCATIONAL SIGNS

Kennel or stable worker

This is likely to be a practical hand, with fingers evenly disposed at their base. The little finger and thumb are typically long. Heart Line rising largely on the Mount of Jupiter and curving slightly. Head Line fairly straight, often with a branch to the Heart Line. Well-developed Mounts of Venus, Upper and Lower Mars, and Jupiter. The Marks of Concern will be an advantage.

Lawyer

Typically, the fingers are evenly disposed with smooth knuckles. Heart Line rising on the Mount of Jupiter, or with a tributary from between the mounts, long, clear, and slightly curving. Head Line long and fairly straight, often with a link to the Heart Line, usually from Head Line Sun to Heart Line Mercury. Life Line firm and long with few marks. Squares are excellent signs, especially when they appear on the Heart and Head Lines, and the Mount of the Sun. The Line of Fate is often absent.

Librarian

The main lines are typically arranged evenly and clearly, without extra marks. Heart Line fairly deeply curving. Head Line tied for some way to the Life Line, then dipping to reach the Mount of the Moon. Clear Line of Fate often present. Well-developed uppermost mounts, especially the Mount of Mercury and of the Moon. Triangles are always a good sign, whether on lines or mounts.

Motor mechanic

These will be practical hands and fingertips. The Heart Line is often short and deeply curved after commencing with tributaries from the Mounts of Jupiter and Saturn. Head Line fairly straight. Life Line firm and clear. Both Girdles of Venus are often present.

Well-developed Mounts are the norm, particulary those of Jupiter, Saturn and Upper Mars.

Novelist

Heart Line probably rising on the Mount of Jupiter with many minor tributaries from the region, running low and curving slightly to the edge of the palm. Head Line often with a multiple fork. Both the Head and the Life Line often have ties from the Mount of Jupiter. The Line of Intuition is often present, running clear and firm. A clear Line of Fate is usually present, often finishing at the Head Line. A Line of Fortune is an excellent addition. There are usually many minor lines. Upper Girdle of Venus is often present.

Nurse

Large, practical hands, often with knobbly knuckles and a narrow, flexible thumb. Heart Line long and fairly low, reaching to the edge of the palm, or upwards-curving around the Mount of Mercury. Head Line often with a link to the Heart Line beneath the Mount of Mercury. A tie sometimes runs from the Heart to the Head Line. The Line of Intuition, when present, is a great advantage. Well-developed Mounts, especially those of Venus, Mercury and Upper Mars. Marks of Concern, Line of Sympathy, and Mark of Mercy are often present and are all advantageous.

Police officer

This is likely to be a practical hand, with firm fingers and long thumbs. Heart line rising on the Mount of Jupiter, then running straight and clear. Head Line fairly straight. Life Line clear and firm, preferably with an Inner Life Line. The Line of Intuition is often present. Well-developed Mounts of Jupiter, Upper and Lower Mars, and Venus. Squares and triangles are beneficial, particularly on the Life Line, the Mount of Jupiter and both Mounts of Mars.

SUMMARY OF VOCATIONAL SIGNS

Politician

These hands are typically large and firm, thumbs long, fingers long and evenly disposed at their base. Heart Line rising on the Mount of Jupiter, running fairly straight to the edge of the palm. Head Line fairly straight. Life Line clear and deep, often with an Inner Life Line. Line of Fate usually strong, straight, and clearly defined. Line of Fortune is important for success in this field. Lines of Influence often reach the Line of Fate from the Mount of the Moon. Rascette clearly marked with the topmost ring well chained and islanded.

Publisher

Heart Line probably rising on the Mount of Jupiter. Head Line fairly straight or forked, with the lower prong reaching to the Mount of the Moon, often with multiple forks. The Line of Intuition, when present, is a great asset. Well-developed Mounts, typically, of Jupiter, Saturn, Sun, Mercury and the Moon. Triangles and squares on the Mounts of Saturn and Mercury are especially propitious.

Radio or television presenter

Announcers' and presenters' hands will tend to be small, thumbs long and knuckles smooth. A deeply curving Heart Line rising on the Mount of Jupiter, Head Line long and clear, dipping to the Mount of the Moon, sometimes forked with the uppermost prong running straight to the Upper Mount of Mars. There is often a link between Heart and Head Lines. A Line of Intuition is helpful. Both Upper and Lower Mounts of Mars and the Mount of the Moon should be well developed.

Salesperson

A good seller's hands will tend to be small, with smooth knuckles. Heart Line rising on the Mount of Jupiter or equally on this and the Mount of Saturn, deeply curving, running upwards towards the Mount of Mercury. Head Line should run fairly straight. There may be ties between the Mount of Jupiter and the Head or Life Line. Upper and Lower Mounts of Mars should be well developed. Line of Intuition is very useful. Triangles are very good signs to have, especially on the Mount of Mercury.

Secretary

Fingerprints typically looped or high-arched. The Heart Line best rising on the Mount of Jupiter with a tributary from between the mounts, running fairly straight, often with a branch to the Head Line. The Head Line should be barely tied to the Life Line and reach to the top of the Mount of the Moon, or forked with the upper prong running fairly straight across the palm. A Line of Intuition is a great advantage. Squares are beneficial, triangles excellent, especially when on the Mounts of Mars.

Social welfare worker

Carers often have a Heart Line that rises between the mounts or with tributaries, one from the Mount of Jupiter and one between, then curving low across the palm and rising to meet the Mount of Mercury. Head Line as a rule forked, one prong reaching into the Mount of the Moon, the other fairly straight. A Line of Intuition is a good aid. Fate Line often rising on, or from within, the Life Line, branching as it approaches the Mount of Saturn. Well-developed Mounts of Venus and the Moon. Marks of Concern and a Line of Sympathy, when present, are great assets.

SUMMARY OF VOCATIONAL SIGNS

Soldier

A firmly practical hand. Heart Line rising equally on the Mounts of Jupiter and Saturn, then running fairly straight. Head Line typically plunging into the Mount of the Moon. Often a wide space between the Head and the Life Lines at their commencement. Life Line clear and deep, usually with an Inner Life Line. Line of Fate an advantage when clearly defined. Line of Intuition important for higher ranks. Well-developed Mounts, especially Venus, Upper and Lower Mars, and Jupiter.

Teacher

Heart Line probably rising on the Mount of Jupiter or with a tributary from between the mounts, long and fairly deeply curving, often circling the Mount of Mercury at its conclusion. Head Line: for arts faculty, best dipping to touch the Mount of the Moon; for science faculty, best straight across the palm. Life Line should be clear and preferably with an Inner Life Line. A Line of Intuition is a great advantage. Well developed Mounts of Jupiter, Sun, Mercury and Mars, all best when marked with triangles.

Veterinary surgeon

Heart Line should rise on the Mount of Jupiter with a tributary from between the mounts, running straight to the edge of the palm. Head Line fairly straight but often forked at the end, the uppermost prong forming a link with the Heart Line. Life Line should be long and strong, preferably with an Inner Life Line. A Line of Intuition is an asset. The Line of Fate should be clear and straight. Marks of Concern and a Line of Sympathy are helpful. Well developed Mounts of Venus, Moon and Upper Mars.

18
POINTS TO CONSIDER WHEN GIVING READINGS

Age and peace of mind

A question commonly asked is: Why do the timescales run out at 70, when it is now commonplace for people to live far longer than this? Well, no doubt palmistry worked just as well in Neolithic times as it does now, and people's lives then were likely to have been short and brutal. Our bodies were designed for a Stone Age lifestyle: for going out to work armed with a club and a spear; for returning home to a cave. It was very much a case of survival of the fittest. No wonder our Life Line frequently fragments and forks around the 45-year mark — and no wonder our Line of Fate frequently reaches its peak at the same age. What seems a young middle age to us would probably have represented a grand old age in those days; thereafter, as long as it continued, healthy life was an unexpected bonus.

According to the Book of Psalms, three-score years and ten is the allotted span for human life on earth. But by the time the psalms were written, people were already well shielded from the animal fate of their forebears. So we have to assume that anything that happens after the age of 70 is simply the consequence of all that has gone before: a fate-free retirement present.

Be tactful about age. Many people are touchy about the subject, and many like to pretend that they are younger than they really are. A few older people may be mortally offended if you cast doubt on their little deception. So, if you suspect that this may be the case, when using the timescales it will help if you can pinpoint

POINTS TO CONSIDER

some important sign by its year, and speak only of years thereafter: 'You had a change of occupation around 1996, and things started looking up after that ...'.

There is one thing that palmists should always bear in mind: Never feel tempted to predict a time of death, preferably not for yourself, and most definitely not for anyone else. It could be the cause of great and completely unnecessary anxiety, besides which, the lines of the hand simply cannot supply accurate information of this nature. The same goes for predictions of accidents, disasters of one kind or another, or even serious failure of enterprises. Never feel tempted to alarm anyone; always project a positive and optimistic frame of mind, supplying reassurance and helpful information whenever possible. Always make your predictions as constructive as you can, so that your subjects will feel good about themselves.

The human psyche is a delicately balanced organism, and very easily upset. The universal law which some people know as karma, works behind the scenes to balance everything out — and we are all interlinked and interbalanced. The same applies whether you believe in karma or not; it is simply the natural law of give and take, cause and effect. If you give the pendulum a push, it will naturally swing back at you. If you knowingly harm somebody — hurt their feelings, cause them distress, wish them ill, undermine their self-confidence, compromise their position in society or business, or generally make them feel less happy and peaceful than they were before — you are adversely affecting this great karmic balance. Whatever your underlying motives, you will have caused a state of imbalance. You may be acting out of ignorance. You may even think you are acting for the good, defending some principle or sense of morality; but that imbalance which you have caused, that extra swing of the pendulum, will automatically become a part of your own inner contents. You will have become spiritually unbalanced. This is not something you would want for yourself, and the easiest way to avoid it is to try to make others feel better instead of worse. If you can help somebody to feel at peace with their own selves, you will be at peace with your own self, and this is good.

All this relates to the question of somebody's long-term, large-scale comfort. But what of their short-term, small-scale feelings? A little planning here will not go amiss. When you know somebody really well, and you both understand each other perfectly, you can both relax and enjoy each other's company, without the need for words or reassurances. It works the other way round, too: if you, and somebody you do not know that well, are both completely relaxed and at ease, you will be that much closer to knowing and understanding each other, and the way you both think and feel. Anything that helps to attain that end is bound to help the palmist give an accurate and sympathetic reading. So, if it is a stranger's hand you are going to read, do what you can first to make them at ease, both with themselves, and with you.

Everyone has a private space, an unseen personal zone which surrounds them like an aura, varying in extent from person to person. If somebody invades our privacy zone for no good reason, we feel uneasy, and it makes us tense and on our guard. So the first rule is: Try not to get too close. If you sit closely, side by side, leaning over to peer at their hands, you cannot help but invade their privacy zone. For this reason, it helps if you can read their hands in reverse, or upside down, opposite to the way in which you are used to seeing your own hands. To familiarise yourself with this technique, turn the book around and study the diagrams until you have become familiar with the way they look with their fingers towards you.

But even when you sit opposite someone, close enough to study their palms, you may still make them feel uneasy, because this face-to-face situation can seem vaguely threatening. It is a confrontational attitude, and this again prevents people relaxing and feeling at ease. So, if you have arranged your 'parlour' with two chairs (comfortable but not too deep — upright chairs with arms are best), and a small table (don't forget to have a table lamp, shaded so as to throw its light down onto the table rather than in your face), place the chairs casually, offset so as to form a triangle with the table. This arrangement is a relaxing compromise between the two extremes: the too-close side by side, and the direct confrontation face-to-face. If your subject wants to move their chair, of course, leave it entirely up to them; let them choose the

POINTS TO CONSIDER

position and the angle, and the degree of confrontation, that pleases them most. They will probably do so quite unconsciously, and feel totally at ease

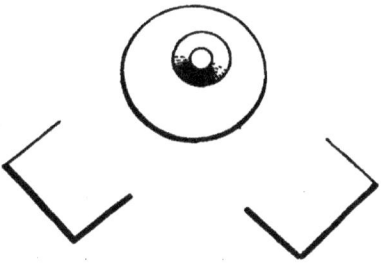

Figure 52

A harmonious seating arrangement

    It will help if you have a large detective-style magnifying glass as one of your 'props', even if you have eagle eyes that can take in every tiny detail; it will make you look more professional, and by scanning the palm carefully you will gain the time needed to identify all the interesting configurations.

    If you own a computer and a digital camera, or just a photocopier, make full use of them to take impressions of as many different hands as you can, and study these at leisure. Alternatively, use a woodcut roller and washable ink, or an inkpad. Prints of your own hands, and those of family and friends, are particularly useful for practice, as you will already know about your own and your family's foibles and characteristics. Work out the timescales for the Life Line, the Lines of Fate and Fortune, and the Marriage Lines, and see what you can discover. Working retrospectively with your own past history, you will find it easy to match the various features with real-life occurrences. Try to remember in particular any emotional upheavals, and the most important things that have happened to you in the past, and try to pinpoint them on your palm. Once you have learnt to plot the course of your own past life in your own hand, you will find it increasingly easy to plot the lives, characters and incidents relating to others in the same way, revealing their past, their present, and their future.

INDEX

accident, risk of 139-140
accountant 160
actor 160
age, respecting 172
aggression 146-147
ambition 147-148
anatomy of the hand 10-11, 13, 14
architect 160
artist 161
assertiveness 148-149
athlete 161

banker 161
builder 162

chain formation *see individual lines*
cheirotype 35-51
chemist 162
childlines 108, 128
church minister 162
clerical officer 163
computer programmer 163
Concern, Marks of 108, 126-128
cook 163
creativity 149-150
cross, *see individual lines and mounts*
  Gambler's 129
  Grand 128
  Mystic 126, 128-129
  Occult 129
crossbars *see individual lines*

death, predictions of 173
depression 150-151
doctor 163-164

Dominance, Lines of 130, 133-134
doubling *see individual lines*
draftsperson 164
driver (lorry or bus) 164

Earth, symbolism of 22-23
engineer 164
Excess, Line of 123-124

faithfulness 152
farmer 165
fashion designer 165
Fate, Line of 88-95
  signs on 94
  timescale on 89-91
fickleness 152-153
fingerprints 49-51
fingers, curve of 42-44
  length of 39
  span 44-46
fingertips 37, 125
forester 165
Fortune, Line of 96-101
  signs on 101
  timescale on 97

Girdle of Venus, Lower 111-112
  Upper 109-110
Great Quadrangle 128
grid *see individual mounts*

hand, size of 38-39
Head Line 67-77
  signs on 77
  tie to Heart Line 75-77
Health, Line of 120-124
  signs on 124

INDEX

Heart Line 53-66
    rising point of 56-57
    signs on 63
    tie to Head Line 64-66
hospital administrator 166
hotel manager 166
hypochondria 120-124

impressions of the hand 175
Influence, Lines of 84-86, 130-135
inheritance 141-145
  Line of 80, 84
introspection 153-154
Intuition, Line of 102-105
    signs on 105
islands *see individual lines*

jealousy 154-155
journalist 166
journeys 136
Jupiter, Mount of 26-27
  symbolism of 22-23

karma, law of 173
kennel worker 167
kindness 155-156
King Line 97
knuckles 39, 125

Lascivia 124
lawyer 167
left hand — right hand 141-145
librarian 167
Life Line 78-87
    signs on 86-87
    timescale on 79-81
lines, primary and secondary 19

Marriage Line 106-119
    signs on 118
    timescale on 107

Mars, Lower Mount of 31
    signs on 32
    symbolism of 22-23
    Upper Mount of 34
    signs on 34
Medical Stigmata 127-128
Mercury, Mount of 29
    signs on 30
    symbolism of 22-23
Mercy, Mark of 126, 127, 128
moodiness 156-157
Moon, Mount of 33
    signs on 33
    symbolism of 22
Morbidity, Mark of 126, 127, 128
motor mechanic 168-169
Mount of Jupiter 26
    signs on 27
    Mars, Lower 31
    signs on 32
    Mars, Upper 34
    signs on 34
    Mercury 29
    signs on 30
    Moon 33
    signs on 33
    Saturn 27
    signs on 28
    Sun 28
    signs on 29
    Venus 30
    signs on 31
mounts, nature of 16, 21, 24-34
Munchausen's syndrome 124

novelist 168
nurse 168

origins of palmistry 9-10

personal zone 174

personality, nature of 12
phalanges 41-42
planetary rulership 22-24
Point of Self 130
police officer 168
politician 169
private space 174
publisher 169

radio announcer 169
Rascette 19-20
   signs on 20
resourcefulness 157-158
Ring of Solomon 126
romantic liaisons 30, 84, 106

salesperson 170
Saturn, Mount of 27
   signs on 28
   symbolism of 22, 24
Scaffold, Sign of the 28, 94
Seal of Solomon 124
secretary 170
self-confidence 159
seven-year stages 81-83
social welfare worker 170
soldier 171
Solomon, Ring of 126
   Seal of 124
square *see individual lines and mounts*
stable worker 167

stamina 34
star *see individual lines and mounts*
streams of consciousness 16-18
Success, Star of 101
Sun Line 96-101
   Mount of 28
     signs on 29
     symbolism of 22-23
Supernal Line 126-129
   Zone 128
Sympathy, Line of 125, 127

teacher 171
television presenter 169
thumbs 42, 46-49
   flexibility of 47
   length of 47
timescales 81-83, 172
Travel Lines 136-140
triangle *see individual lines and mounts*
twins, studies on 12

Venus, Mount of 30
   signs on 31
   Rising Star of 31, 112
   Setting Star of 31, 112, 113
   symbolism of 22-23
veterinary surgeon 171

warning signs 139-140

www.ingramcontent.com/pod-product-compliance
Lightning Source LLC
Chambersburg PA
CBHW060525090426
42735CB00011B/2372